Timothy V. Rasinski & Melissa Ch

THE
MEGABOOK
OF
FLUENCY

Strategies and Texts
to Engage All Readers

SCHOLASTIC

*To my mom, Lark Cheesman, who left me this year but whose memory will always sing inside me,
"a sightless song."*
—MCS

To all the wonderful teachers I have met and have had the honor to work with over the past 40+ years. So much of what is in this book comes from you. Thank you. Keep a poem in your pocket and a song in your heart!
—TVR

Credits

Photos ©: back cover: Kevin Carlson; 109: Steve Debenport/iStockphoto; 238: PeopleImages/iStockphoto; 247: Hulton Archive/Getty Images; 256: duncan1890/iStockphoto; 260: Rolls Press/Popperfoto/Getty Images; 276: PeopleImages/iStockphoto; 277: FatCamera/iStockphoto; 302: Design Pics/Ashley Armstrong/Media Bakery; all other photos by Mark Lipczynski for Scholastic.

Publisher: Lois Bridges
Editorial director: Sarah Longhi
Development editor: Raymond Coutu
Production editor: Danny Miller
Art director: Brian LaRossa
Interior and cover designer: Kyle Kirkup

ISBN-13: 978-1-338-25701-4
ISBN-10: 1-338-25701-3

3 4 5 6 7 8 9 10   14   27 26 25 24 23 22 21 20 19

⚠ Text pages printed on 30% PCW recycled paper.

Acknowledgments

Our book would be a mere tangle of words and ideas if not for the team of muses that turned it into a beautiful resource for teachers. Thank you to Lois Bridges for being our advocate, and for the foresight and vision of seeing the end of our tangle: to craft our ideas into a tangible resource. Ray Coutu, thank you for your unmatched competence to develop while staying true to the integrity of the content. A special thank you to Brian LaRossa for taking the time to listen to every suggestion and idea and cultivate it into the direction of the endless forms of art throughout the book. Our gratitude also goes to Sarah Longhi for helping with all the details of the book, Danny Miller, our masterful copy editor, and Kyle Kirkup for the beautiful interior of the book. We'd like to thank principal Randy Yates of Village Prep Cliffs in Cleveland, along with reading coaches Kelly Foerg and Kelly Greene for letting us into their classrooms. Finally, we wish to acknowledge and thank poets David Harrison and Robert Pottle, who were so generous in allowing us to use some of their fabulous poetry in our book.

From Tim:

I would like to thank Melissa for her foresight in first visualizing this book and for her perseverance in seeing it through to completion. In 2015, I had just made a presentation on reading fluency at the Arizona Reading Association conference when Melissa came up to me to suggest that we take the ideas in my *Fluent Reader* (2nd edition) book and cast them as actionable lessons that teachers can employ with children. And so we did! Melissa truly is a teachers' teacher. I am so pleased and honored to have spent my career associated with great educators like her. My wife, Kathy, also deserves a shout-out and a good deal of thanks as well. For over 42 years she has kept me grounded on what matters most in life—family, friends, and doing good in the world.

From Melissa:

I'd like to thank first and foremost Tim, whom I call the "King of Fluency" and who will forever be a legend in education with his love for words, songs, and children. You have inspired me over the last 15 years to see that with the right knowledge, foundational reading teaching can be fun and easy, a win-win for teachers and students. Thank you for taking a chance on me. To Deb Junkes, who believed in me long before I did and whom I have been blessed to have as a colleague and friend during my career. To my husband, David, and my children, Londyn, Davaya, and Jackson, who supported me and allowed me to sacrifice wife and mom time for career time. And finally, for all my students throughout my career—the passionate ones, the struggling ones, the motivated ones, the naughty ones—you have all made me only fall more and more in love with the art of teaching.

CONTENTS

Videos and downloadables are available at **Scholastic.com/ FluencyResources.**

INTRODUCTION

"Once you learn to read, you will be forever free."

—**Frederick Douglass**

It was one of those years. Beth Thomas, a very dedicated third-grade teacher, knew she had her work cut out for her. Of the 24 students in her class, over half struggled with reading. Although nearly all students were proficient at word decoding, thanks to a new approach to phonics instruction that seemed to be working well, most of the strugglers did it in a slow and monotone manner. They expressed little joy or confidence in their reading as they labored from one word to another. To make matters worse, these students also struggled in comprehending what they read. When asked to retell a passage just read, for example, few could offer more than a few facts from the passage.

From previous professional development presentations that she had attended and her own professional reading, Beth knew that a lack of reading fluency was likely the problem. Even some of her good readers seemed to exhibit difficulties in fluency. So she decided that fluency instruction was just what her students needed in the coming year.

At the same time, Beth was not comfortable with the "speed read" approaches to fluency instruction that were in vogue at the time. Timed readings that required students to practice a short passage repeatedly for the primary purpose of reaching a prescribed reading speed were less-than-authentic reading activities. Were there other more authentic ways to provide fluency instruction that her students would find engaging and effective?

Fortunately for Beth, she began to think about the true nature of fluent speech and fluent reading. It's not speaking or reading fast; rather, fluency is speaking and reading with expression that reflects and adds to the meaning of the oral or written message. Beth began looking for texts and activities that lent themselves to expressive oral reading. She found poetry, songs, scripts, famous speeches, and other such texts that beg for expressive reading. And, she found ways for her students to perform these texts in real ways—poetry coffee houses, Readers' Theater festivals, classroom sing-alongs, and so forth. Her students began to beg to do more and more fluency work. It was the one of the best parts of the school day. Moreover, the authentic reading practice scenarios that Beth created led to significant improvements in her students' fluency and overall reading achievement in a matter of weeks! Beth is a believer in the importance of fluency and authentic fluency instruction.

Teachers across the country face Beth's predicament all the time. Reading fluency is a critical goal for reading success. Yet, the approaches for teaching fluent reading are often divorced from real reading. Teachers are looking for approaches that go beyond increasing students' speed. This book is aimed at providing you, a dedicated and knowledgeable teacher, with smart alternatives.

What Is Fluency? All EARS!

Fluency is the ability to read with Expression, Automatic word recognition, Rhythm and phrasing, and Smoothness (EARS). Fluency has traditionally been neglected in reading programs (Allington, 1983), and when it has been embraced, it is often misunderstood (Rasinski, 2006, 2012). So having a good grasp of reading fluency is certainly an appropriate place to start.

We often think of the act of reading as involving two major competencies: word decoding (phonics) and comprehension. Fluency is, in a sense, a critical link between those two competencies (Rasinski, 2010). Fluency itself is made up of two subcomponents: word recognition automaticity and prosody, or expressive reading.

Automatic and Smooth Word Recognition

Automaticity and smoothness in word recognition is critical because it minimizes the cognitive energy needed to recognize many words, thus enabling the reader to focus on the more important task of comprehending the text. While reading this paragraph, you are likely exhibiting word recognition automaticity. As you read, you can accurately decode the words. In fact, most of the words you are encountering you are recognizing instantly and holistically, without applying any phonic analyses. Most of the words we encounter as proficient adult readers are read this way—as sight words we recognize automatically.

Beth's struggling readers were able to decode words accurately, but not automatically. They had to use their phonics skills to analyze many of the words they encountered. This resulted in two outcomes. First, their reading was excessively slow because of the phonic analyses required of so many of the words they encountered. Second, because they had to invest so much cognitive energy into the decoding task, comprehension was impaired. Word recognition automaticity is critical for proficient reading. Research has demonstrated a robust correlation between word recognition automaticity and reading comprehension (Rasinski, Reutzel, Chard, & Linan-Thompson, 2011).

Expression and Rhythm

The second subcomponent of fluency, which is often overlooked, is prosody—or expressive reading with appropriate rhythm and phrasing that reflect the meaning of the text. Prosodic reading is fluency's link to comprehension. In order for readers to read a passage with good expression and rhythm, they have to be comprehending the meaning of the passage. And, conversely, reading with appropriate expression and rhythm enhances readers' comprehension of the passage's meaning (as well as the comprehension of anyone listening to the reading).

Because silent reading proficiency is often viewed as the gold standard for reading instruction over oral reading proficiency, or more precisely, expressive oral reading proficiency, it is sometimes overlooked by curriculum developers.

The Vocabulary of Fluency

Fluency: The ability to read with Expression, Automatic word recognition, Rhythm and phrasing, and Smoothness.

E **Expression**	**Prosody**	Expression used in reading that reflects and expands on the meaning of the text.
	Intonation	Fluctuation of voice in the strength of pitch and volume to match the meaning of the text.
	Tone	Reading to show an emotion or feeling.
	Monotone	Having single or unvaried tone in a way that expression doesn't match the meaning of the text.
	Stress	Emphasis on particular words or phrases as one would do in conversational speech.
A **Automatic Word Recognition**	**Automaticity**	The ability of a reader to recognize/decode words in text accurately and effortlessly or automatically.
	Pace/Rate	The pace or speed at which the reader can move through the text. Pacing is a good way to assess automaticity.
	WCPM	Words Correct Per Minute—the rate or pace at which a student reads.
R **Rhythm and Phrasing**	**Phrasing/ Chunking**	Reading in meaningful phrases or word chunks instead of word by word.
	Pausing	Using punctuation as a guide to when to pause while reading.
S **Smoothness**	**Accuracy**	The ability to accurately recognize or decode words regardless of rate.
	Self-correct	The ability of a reader to recognize an error in her/his reading and fix/repair it.

Why Is Fluency Important?

The research of the past two decades demonstrates quite clearly a robust correlation between expressive oral reading and silent reading comprehension (Rasinski, Reutzel, Chard, & Linan-Thompson, 2011). That is, students who read orally with good expression are more likely to comprehend deeply when reading silently.

So we see fluency as this critical bridge between word recognition and comprehension. If students are unable to develop that bridge, they will likely have difficulty in achieving necessary levels of comprehension when reading.

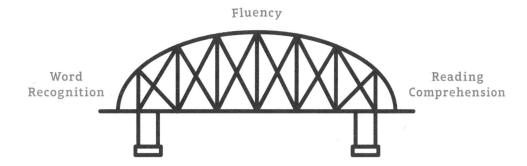

Furthermore, a number of studies have found strong connections between reading fluency and general measures of reading achievement, including comprehension (Chard, Vaughn, & Tyler, 2002; Kuhn & Stahl, 2003; Kuhn, Schwanenflugel, & Meisinger, 2010; National Reading Panel, 2000; Rasinski, 2010; Rasinski, Reutzel, Chard, & Linan-Thompson, 2011). Moreover, these and other studies have documented the power of reading fluency in primary, intermediate, middle school, and high school students (e.g., Rasinski, Padak, McKeon, Krug-Wilfong, Friedauer, & Heim, 2005; Rasinski, Rikli, & Johnston, 2009). Higher levels of fluency are associated with more proficient reading, while low levels of fluency point to lower levels of reading proficiency.

A growing number of studies have examined the effects of authentic fluency instruction. By "authentic," we mean real reading of real texts for real purposes, to communicate meaning. We contrast authentic fluency instruction with programs that tend to require readers to increase their reading speed. The studies of authentic fluency instruction confirm that the type of instruction we describe in this book not only leads to improved fluency, but also to higher levels of reading proficiency, including comprehension, and also greater levels of interest and motivation for reading for all readers (Rasinski, 2010, 2012), especially those who are experiencing difficulty (Rasinski, 2017).

Despite the recognition of fluency's importance, many students struggle with it. A study of elementary students identified as experiencing difficulty in reading and recommended for intervention found that fluency was their greatest challenge (Rasinski & Padak, 1998). Another study of elementary students who performed poorly on a state-mandated reading proficiency test found that 75 to 90 percent of the students exhibited significant difficulties in one or more aspects of reading fluency (Duke, Pressley, & Hilden, 2004; Valencia & Buly, 2004). And, difficulties are not limited to younger students. If fluency concerns are not addressed early, during the foundational years, it is likely that those concerns will find their way into the middle school and high school grades. Indeed, several studies have found that fluency is associated with reading achievement beyond the elementary grades (Paige, Rasinski, & Magpuri-Lavell, 2012; Paige, Rasinski, Magpuri-Lavell, & Smith, 2014; Rasinski, Padak, McKeon, Krug-Wilfong, Friedauer, & Heim, 2005). Furthermore, because fluency is a foundational competency, difficulties in fluency can also lead to difficulties in content areas that rely heavily on reading.

Given the importance of fluency and the fact that fluency difficulties are widespread among students of all ages, effective fluency instruction and intervention are essential to improving the overall reading achievement of those students, as well as their achievement in the content areas. That is what this book is all about.

Is Fluency Foundational to Reading Proficiency? Yes, the Standards Say So!

Over the past several years, much attention has been focused on learning standards for reading success—the Common Core State Standards for the English Language Arts (National Governors Association and Council of Chief State School Officers, 2016), as well as standards developed by individual states and local school districts. Most standards documents suggest that higher and more sophisticated levels of reading are built on a solid foundation of reading fluency. Without a solid foundation, a building cannot stand; without a solid foundation in reading fluency, other reading competencies, such as comprehension and close reading, cannot develop. It is critical, then, that we help all our students so they may move on to higher levels of reading achievement.

But it's not just the standards that tell us that reading fluency is important. A number of scientifically-based studies have demonstrated that fluency instruction leads to overall improvement in fluency and comprehension for students in the elementary, middle, and secondary grades (Rasinski, Reutzel, Chard, & Linan-Thompson, 2011), especially for students who struggle in reading (Stevens, Walter, & Vaughn, 2017).

What Are the Building Blocks of Reading Fluency?

If reading fluency is the foundation for reading success, what instructional building blocks can we use to lay that foundation? We identify several major approaches to building fluency that you can use to move students to more fluent reading. All the activities in this book incorporate one or more of these building blocks. (For a more complete discussion of these approaches, see *The Fluent Reader, Second Edition* [Rasinski, 2010]).

Modeled Fluent Reading

If we want students to move toward fluency in reading, we have to give them a sense of what fluency is. The best way to do that is for them to hear fluent reading often. We need to read to students regularly. Moreover, we should take time to discuss why our reading is fluent and how fluent reading makes it easier for listeners to understand and enjoy the reading.

Supportive or Assisted Reading

Simply listening to a fluent reader will not make a student a fluent reader. They need to engage in fluent reading themselves. However, not all students can read a text fluently on their own—some need support and assistance. Supportive or assisted reading simply means that a student reads a passage while listening to a reading of the same passage.

Supportive or assisted reading can take a variety of forms. Students may read chorally as part of a group. Or they may read with a more fluent partner such as a teacher, parent, classroom aide, older student, or even a classmate. Something special happens when a less fluent reader reads a text the best he or she can and simultaneously hears a more fluent reading of the same text: a movement toward more fluent and meaningful reading. Researcher Keith Topping found that regular assisted (paired) reading could accelerate a student's overall reading progress by a factor of three or more. That is, students who previously were making a half-month's progress in reading for every month of instruction could be expected to make one-and-a-half-months' progress when assisted reading was included in the curriculum (Topping, 1987a, 1987b, 1989).

The student does not always have to read with another person. He or she can read a text while simultaneously listening to a prerecorded version of the same text. We call this audio-assisted reading, and the recording can be an audio file (e.g., an MP3 file) stored on your computer or other device. As with other forms of supportive or assisted reading, the research into audio-assisted reading points to improvements in students' fluency and overall reading proficiency (Rasinski, 2010; Rasinski, Reutzel, Chard, & Linan-Thompson, 2011).

Reading Practice: Wide Reading

Becoming fluent at anything, from walking to reading, requires practice. For most students (and adults), wide reading is the most common form of practice that leads to growth (Kuhn, et al., 2006). Wide reading simply means reading a text once, perhaps discussing it and/or doing some extension activity related to it, and then moving on to a new text—in other words, reading one text after another. This form of authentic reading practice is important because we want students to read as much as possible in order to develop critical competencies.

Reading Practice: Repeated Reading

For students who struggle to attain fluency, wide reading is not enough. These students need to read one text a few times until they are able to achieve fluency. In other words, they need repeated reading. A more common name often associated with repeated reading is rehearsal. Interestingly, the Common Core State Standards refer to repeated reading as close reading.

Research has demonstrated that each time students read a text, their reading improves on many fronts: word recognition, accuracy, automaticity, expression, and comprehension (Dowhower, 1994; Samuels, 1979). More importantly, when they move on to a brand-new text to read, their gains "stick." In other words, the benefit from practicing one passage repeatedly carries over to passages they've never before read.

The key to successful repeated reading is making it authentic (Rasinski, 2012). In many current programs for and approaches to developing fluency, students are asked to read a text repeatedly until they achieve a specified reading speed or rate (since reading rate is a way to measure one aspect of fluency). But this approach to repeated reading lacks authenticity. Who in real life repeatedly reads a passage for the purpose of reading it quickly?

We believe that authenticity starts with rehearsal. Any type of performance for an audience, whether it is giving a speech, reciting a poem, singing a song, or acting in a play, requires rehearsal. Rehearsal is not about reading quickly, but about communicating with meaning for the enjoyment of a listening audience. This is the type of repeated reading that students will find not only authentic, but also highly engaging and motivating.

Rhythm and Phrasing

If you think about it, a hallmark characteristic of a less fluent reader is reading in a word-by-word manner, without concern for meaning making. These readers may be able to read the words of a text correctly, but the staccato-like delivery minimizes the meaning that is communicated to the listener. Although we might think of the word as the basic unit of meaning in a text, it's really in the phrasing where meaning is lodged. What do words such as *the, of, to, and,* or *if* mean by themselves? Not much. But when they become part of a phrase, their meaning becomes clear. Fluent readers read in meaningful phrases; struggling readers very often read word-by-word. Helping our less fluent readers move away from word-by-word reading to more phrased and meaning-filled reading is an important goal for instruction and well worth the effort (Rasinski, Yildirim, & Nageldinger, 2011).

What Makes a Quality Fluency Activity?

While not all effective fluency activities are designed or structured the same, they do share common elements and characteristics (Rasinski, 2005). Here are a few:

Quality Texts

Try to find texts that have a good voice and phrasing and are meant to be read orally with expression. Texts such as poetry, scripts, and narratives work very well for developing fluency.

Oral Reading

The text must be read aloud. Fluency practice should be oral so students can hear what good reading sounds like. And keep in mind, authentic practice in oral reading will not only improve fluency but also silent reading skills.

Feedback

Students should receive feedback. Sometimes feedback comes from their own observations as they tap into their metacognitive skills and think about how they sound as they read. Sometimes feedback comes from you, the class, or a classmate. In either case, students should evaluate their oral readings. They can use the Student Fluency Evaluation forms at the back of this book (and available for download at Scholastic.com/FluencyResources) to get a sense of how they're progressing.

Repetition

For fluency to improve, repeated reading is strongly encouraged. Emphasis should be aimed primarily at providing practice reading the text with appropriate expression that reflects its meaning.

Motivation

Most fluency activities are naturally engaging and even fun. Songs, poems, chants, and other rhythmic texts are all motivational because there is an element of playfulness to them; they often beg to be read and performed aloud. And when students read them over and over, they become successful, which can be motivational in and of itself. But for the students to *want* to read the text repeatedly, the text should be engaging. It is a good idea to provide students with an audience of even just one person for their reading who can provide positive feedback.

Top Benefits of Fluency Instruction and Activities

- Improve not only oral reading fluency, but also silent reading fluency.

- Promote expressive reading.

- Highlight the richness of words in quality literature.

- Increase students' vocabulary.

- Help students express meaning through nuances in prosody.

- Improve classroom community and climate.

- Unify all types of learners in a community experience (English language learners, struggling students, etc.).

- Increase reading time at school.

- Boost student confidence.

- Increase comprehension (paying attention to punctuation, connotation of words through expression, etc.).

- Require rehearsal, an authentic form of repeated readings.

- Lead to improved word recognition accuracy and automaticity.

What Is the Best Way to Assess Fluency?

Using the Multidimensional Fluency Scale

Understanding reading fluency and understanding students who may require additional instruction in fluency require an understanding of how fluency can be measured. As we mentioned earlier, fluency is made up of two subcomponents: automaticity and prosody. Within these subcomponents, fluency can be broken down into four steps we call EARS (Expression, Automatic word recognition, Rhythm and phrasing, and Smoothness) and then measured using the Multidimensional Fluency Scale. Fluency is best measured both qualitatively and quantitatively, so all dimensions should be considered.

We know that fluency isn't all about speed, but it's a part of it, because slowing down to decode negatively impacts comprehension. Each section of EARS is measured by students reading one text, and then you choose the closest match to the choices in the Scale. For the "A" in EARS, Automatic Word Recognition, a simple protocol for assessing speed, or words per minute, can also be used. The basic steps are listening to a child read a text of 100 to 200 words at grade level for one minute. While the student reads, the teacher keeps track of errors and counts the words read in one minute minus errors. This number is the Oral Reading Fluency (ORF) score and is reported in Words Correct Per Minute (WCPM). Specific details and texts

Multidimensional Fluency Scale

	4 Excelling	3 Proficient	2 Approaching	1 Developing
E Expression · expression matches meaning · varied volume, intonation, and tone · reads with confidence · natural-sounding	· consistently uses expression through varied intonation, volume, and tone to match meaning · reads with confidence · is natural-sounding and easy to understand	· mostly uses expression by sometimes varying intonation, volume, and tone to match meaning · shows confidence but inconsistently · is mostly natural-sounding and easy to understand	· attempts expression, but is inconsistent and often does not match the meaning · lacks confidence, reads quietly · primarily focuses on saying the words correctly	· pays minimal or no attention to expression · reads in a quiet and monotone voice · reads words as if simply to get them out
A Automatic Word Recognition · reads automatically · reads effortlessly · pace matches text (rate)	· reads nearly all words automatically and effortlessly · uses a pace that is consistently conversational and appropriate for the nature of the text · number of words read per minute matches grade-level requirement. See "Target Fluency Ranges" table on page 16	· reads most words automatically and effortlessly · uses a mixture of conversational and slow reading · number of words read per minute meets grade-level requirement. See "Target Fluency Ranges" table on page 16	· does not read most words automatically and has to stop to recognize words · reads at a moderately slow pace · number of words read per minute is below grade-level requirement. See "Target Fluency Ranges" table on page 16	· does not read words automatically and has to stop frequently to recognize words · reads at an excessively slow and laborious pace · number of words read is well below grade-level requirement. See "Target Fluency Ranges" table on page 16
R Rhythm and Phrasing · reads phrase-by-phrase chunks · attention to punctuation with intonation and pauses · easy to listen to	· reads primarily in phrases, chunks, and sentence units · pays attention to intonation and pauses at punctuation consistently and accurately	· reads with some choppiness, but is generally able to go phrase by phrase · pays attention to intonation and usually pauses at punctuation consistently and accurately	· reads in two- and three-word phrases frequently · reads with choppiness · often exhibits improper intonation and pauses at punctuation	· reads word by word frequently · reads in a monotonic manner · shows little sense of phrase boundaries · exhibits improper intonation and pauses at punctuation
S Smoothness · smooth-sounding with flow · accurate word recognition · minimal hesitations · self-corrects	· reads nearly all words accurately · reads smoothly, with minimal hesitations · has few word and structure difficulties and corrects quickly	· reads most words accurately · breaks occasionally from smoothness and hesitates · has a few difficulties with specific words and/or structures, but they do not impede overall flow	· struggles to read words accurately · pauses and hesitates frequently at "rough spots" in text, which disrupts the overall flow	· requires frequent assistance for inaccuracies: long pauses, insertions, mispronunciation, omissions, false starts, sound-outs, repetitions · is unaware of mistakes

(See full-sized Fluency Scale on page 316. You can also download it at Scholastic.com/FluencyResources.)

for assessment can be found in *3-Minute Reading Assessments: Word Recognition, Fluency & Comprehension* (Rasinski & Padak, 2005).

Compare the score against the norms in the table below (Rasinski & Padak, 2005). Students who generally score within the ranges indicated in the table can be considered to be making adequate progress in fluency. Students near the lower end or below the ranges indicated in the table below should be considered for fluency intervention. Students scoring above the ranges in the table may be reading too quickly to comprehend the text adequately.

Target Fluency Ranges as Measured by Words Correct Per Minute (WCPM)			
Grade	Fall	Winter	Spring
1		20–50	30–90 wcpm
2	30–80	50–100	70–130
3	50–110	70–120	80–140
4	70–120	80–130	90–140
5	80–130	90–140	100–150
6	90–140	100–150	110–160
7	100–150	110–160	120–170
8	110–160	120–180	130–180

This assessment can be administered regularly (e.g., once per month) to determine if students are making good progress. You may choose to have students who are reading well below grade level read a passage that more closely matches their instructional reading level. However, because the norms in the table are based on students reading material at their assigned grade level, you will need to use your professional judgment to interpret the scores. This is a data-based approach for keeping track of reading progress in your classroom.

Scoring the Multidimensional Fluency Scale

In a matter of just a few minutes, using the Multidimensional Fluency Scale, you can get a good sense of how your students are doing in fluency. The scores will range from 4 to 16. Here are some score ranges to give you a sense of your students' performance:

Score of 4–6: Student is underperforming in fluency levels.
Score of 7–11: Student is approaching grade-level norms of fluency.
Score of 12–16: Student is on or above grade level in fluency.

This book is designed in a way that you can identify concerns based on the four dimensions of the Multidimensional Fluency Scale and identify areas where students need instructional support and intervention. You can then choose strategies that will help develop those skills individually, in small groups, or as a class. Many strategies and activities can also be copied and sent home for parents to help their child one-on-one.

Why Is Fluency Sometimes Viewed as "Not Hot"?

Despite a growing recognition of the importance of reading fluency in students' reading development, that message is often lost because of how it is typically understood and taught (Samuels, 2007; Rasinski, 2012). As mentioned earlier, word recognition automaticity is generally measured by reading speed. If readers are able to recognize words in text automatically, it follows that they will be able to read at a faster pace and read better than readers who can't. This connection between word recognition automaticity and reading achievement has led to instructional practices aimed primarily at increasing students' reading rate. As such, "fluency instruction" often looks like this:

- Student reads a passage as quickly as possible.
- Teacher times the student's reading—how many seconds it takes to read the passage.
- Student reads the passage a second time, trying to outdo his or her time on the first reading.
- Student continues reading the same passage repeatedly until a target reading rate is achieved.
- The process is repeated with new passages for the student to read.

While we acknowledge that word recognition automaticity is highly correlated to reading speed, we do not feel that reading speed improves word recognition automaticity. Rather, the opposite is often true; as students become more automatic in their word recognition, two things occur: first, reading speed increases, and second, reading achievement improves. Reading speed is the result of automaticity, not the cause. Because of the type of "fluency instruction" described earlier, you can easily see how students begin to view reading as a contest in which they try to read as quickly as possible, without regard for comprehending what they are reading.

Many teachers have become aware of this misconception and, as a result, have dropped fluency instruction from their reading curriculum. Although we applaud teachers who resist ill-conceived methods of instruction, fluency is too important to ignore.

Another problem with fluency is associated with prosody. Readers who read orally with good expression that captures the text's meaning tend also to be proficient silent readers. Prosodic reading is often missing from fluency instruction, as we see it, for three reasons. First, if fluency instruction is improving reading speed, little emphasis can be placed on prosody. Indeed, expressive reading suggests that there are places where a reader needs to slow down. And, of course, reading with expression requires reading at a conversational pace, not a fast pace.

Second, in most classrooms today, the goal of the reading curriculum is for students to become proficient in silent reading. Therefore, oral reading, by default, receives less attention, and it follows that prosody in oral reading receives little to no attention.

Third, prosody is difficult to measure objectively. Assessments are dependent on a teacher's or other listener's judgment of what makes reading expressive. Although we have found great consistency in how teachers assess prosody, the argument can be made that how one teacher assesses prosody in oral reading may be significantly different from the way other teachers do. If such assessments vary greatly, the reliability and value of the assessment (and any instruction that may follow) is questionable.

Why *The Megabook of Fluency?*

Richard Allington called fluency "the neglected goal of the reading program" (1983). In many ways, fluency continues to be not only neglected, but also deeply misunderstood or, at best, marginalized. We think that is a huge mistake. We do not advocate using the instructional methods described in the previous section, but rather effective, engaging, and authentic methods that build word recognition automaticity (not speed) and prosodic or expressive reading. In this book, you will find a wealth of motivating oral and silent reading strategies that we have found through our own work to be effective, engaging, and authentic in promoting reading fluency. Not only will these strategies promote fluency, they will also help you create students who use fluency for its intended purpose: to comprehend the texts they read (Rasinski, 2010).

The strategies will move your students to more meaningful reading. We hope you will adapt them to meet the specific needs of your students. We also hope you will be inspired to use them as templates or models for your own fluency activities.

Although we present the strategies for use in the classroom or clinic, they can easily be adapted to be used at home. Indeed, our experience has been that many parents find these strategies a great way to make reading a part of family life. As you peruse the book, our greatest hope is that the strategies are just a starting point for making fluency instruction an integral, enjoyable, and effective part of your overall reading curriculum.

A Close-Up Look at a Strategy Page

The strategy sections in each chapter begin with a page that spells out clearly everything you need to do to plan for, carry out, and extend instruction. Most of those strategy pages are immediately followed by student work pages that can be photocopied and/or downloaded at Scholastic.com/FluencyResources. All essential materials are provided!

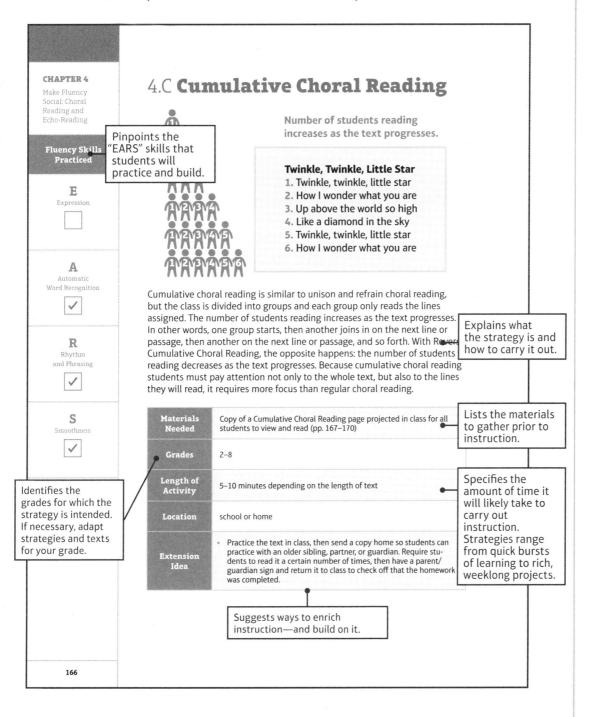

CHAPTER 4
Make Fluency Social: Choral Reading and Echo-Reading

Fluency Skills Practiced

E
Expression

A
Automatic Word Recognition
✓

R
Rhythm and Phrasing
✓

S
Smoothness
✓

Pinpoints the "EARS" skills that students will practice and build.

Identifies the grades for which the strategy is intended. If necessary, adapt strategies and texts for your grade.

4.C Cumulative Choral Reading

Number of students reading increases as the text progresses.

Twinkle, Twinkle, Little Star
1. Twinkle, twinkle, little star
2. How I wonder what you are
3. Up above the world so high
4. Like a diamond in the sky
5. Twinkle, twinkle, little star
6. How I wonder what you are

Cumulative choral reading is similar to unison and refrain choral reading, but the class is divided into groups and each group only reads the lines assigned. The number of students reading increases as the text progresses. In other words, one group starts, then another joins in on the next line or passage, then another on the next line or passage, and so forth. With Reverse Cumulative Choral Reading, the opposite happens: the number of students reading decreases as the text progresses. Because cumulative choral reading students must pay attention not only to the whole text, but also to the lines they will read, it requires more focus than regular choral reading.

Explains what the strategy is and how to carry it out.

Materials Needed	Copy of a Cumulative Choral Reading page projected in class for all students to view and read (pp. 167–170)
Grades	2–8
Length of Activity	5–10 minutes depending on the length of text
Location	school or home
Extension Idea	• Practice the text in class, then send a copy home so students can practice with an older sibling, partner, or guardian. Require students to read it a certain number of times, then have a parent/guardian sign and return it to class to check off that the homework was completed.

Lists the materials to gather prior to instruction.

Specifies the amount of time it will likely take to carry out instruction. Strategies range from quick bursts of learning to rich, weeklong projects.

Suggests ways to enrich instruction—and build on it.

166

Videos and
downloadables
are available at
**Scholastic.com/
FluencyResources.**

CHAPTER 1

Begin Early: Reading Fluency in the Primary Grades (and Beyond)

"A poem begins in delight and ends in wisdom."

—**Robert Frost**

Children become fluent early in life. Babies express meaning in the ways they babble, coo, and cry. Parents can easily tell what their baby might want or need simply by the tone of his or her voice or the nature of the cry. Indeed, well before being able to speak conventionally, children can express themselves fluently to convey meaning. Oral language is, after all, the foundation of reading—children enter reading as potent language learners.

During kindergarten and first grade, we want their early understandings about fluency to move with them into conventional reading. As we stated in the introduction, words in print alone don't just convey meaning; the ways those words are expressed do, too. We can help young children develop reading fluency in a number of ways, especially by telling them stories and reading to them. When we do this, we use our voices naturally and expressively to enhance whatever story we're telling or text we're reading. Children listen to how we phrase words, use inflection in our voice, and read smoothly and rhythmically. All this is part of being a good reader. And when children are exposed to it in kindergarten and first grade, it can have a dramatic effect on how they apply those skills themselves when they begin to decode.

Additionally, when telling stories and reading to children, we should take time to talk with them about *how* we use our voice to help convey meaning to develop an awareness of fluent expressive reading. After modeling fluency for students, we can have the children read songs, rhymes, poems, patterned texts, and other texts that are easy for them to read and have features that support fluent reading—texts that are not only effective and joyful introductions to fluency, but also to reading itself. The brevity, rhythm, rhyme, and in many cases the melody of song, rhymes, poems, and patterned texts are perfect for our emerging readers.

In kindergarten and first grade, we want to set the stage for reading fluency of all texts. This chapter provides you with easy-to-implement activities and texts for doing just that.

Strategies

**Fluency Skills
Practiced**

E
Expression

A
Automatic
Word Recognition

R
Rhythm
and Phrasing

S
Smoothness

1.A **Wordless Picture Book "Readings"**

"Read aloud" wordless picture books, demonstrating how to create the story with illustrations and your expressive voice. Discuss with students how you use your voice to add to the meaning of the story as well as to boost their enjoyment of it. Then, have students "read aloud" their own wordless picture books and create the story. Students may naturally "read" with expression. If they don't, read with them and model expressive reading. Tell them that such reading is important because it makes the text more meaningful and satisfying. Students can also create dialogue for the characters, using expression to match the intended meaning in the story.

Materials Needed	Wordless picture books, such as: *Chalk* by Bill Thomson, *Flotsam* by David Wiesner, *Fossil* by Bill Thomson, *Good Night, Gorilla* by Peggy Rathmann, *Pancakes for Breakfast* by Tomie dePaola, *Re-Zoom* by Istvan Banyai, *The Lion and the Mouse* by Jerry Pinkney, *The Red Book* by Barbara Lehman, *Thunderstorm* by Arthur Geisert, *Tuesday* by David Wiesner, *Zoom* by Istvan Banyai
Grades	K–5
Length of Activity	20 minutes
Location	school or home
Extension Ideas	• After reading/telling the story once, try reading it (or a portion of it) in a different mood and voice (e.g., as if excited, as if in a hurry, as if sad). Talk with students about how your mood affected how you read the text. • After reading certain lines to students, ask them to "read" those lines themselves, modeling their own expression after yours.

1.B **Storytelling With Puppets**

**Fluency Skills
Practiced**

Provide puppets, or have students create puppets on their own or in groups, and use them to retell well-known stories. Then, students practice and perform a brief puppet show for the class as you work with groups to demonstrate and develop expressive dialogue. (For example, if they're performing "The Three Little Pigs," the student playing the wolf may say the line, "Little pig, little pig, let me in!" loudly with a growl, just as the wolf might.)

Materials Needed	Preprinted puppets, or materials to make puppets Common familiar stories, easily found on the Internet, such as: • "The Little Red Hen" • "Little Red Riding Hood" • "The Three Bears" • "The Three Little Pigs" • "The Ugly Duckling"
Grades	K–2
Length of Activity	30 minutes
Location	school or home

E
Expression

A
Automatic
Word Recognition

R
Rhythm
and Phrasing

S
Smoothness

**Fluency Skills
Practiced**

E

Expression

A

Automatic
Word Recognition

R

Rhythm
and Phrasing

S

Smoothness

1.C Read Aloud With Emergent Readers

Read aloud picture books so students hear words read correctly and learn what good readers do. In the process, they become aware of the importance of phrasing, expression, and pacing of a reading. Picking books in which those skills can be showcased is key. See suggestions below.

Materials Needed	For strategies used with younger children, we have chosen books with repeated phrases so children can read along and predict what comes next. These include books such as: Frog and Toad series by Arnold Lobel: *Days With Frog and Toad, Frog and Toad All Year, Frog and Toad Are Friends, Frog and Toad Together* (Focus on how to read dialogue.) Diary of a… series by Doreen Cronin: *Diary of a Fly, Diary of a Worm, Diary of a Spider* (Focus on funny antics that show emotion and require expression.) David series by David Shannon: *No, David!, David Gets in Trouble, David Goes to School* (Focus on using punctuation to read with expression.) Alexander series by Judith Viorst: *Alexander and the Terrible, Horrible, No Good, Very Bad Day; Alexander Who Used to Be Rich Last Sunday; Alexander Who's Not (Do You Hear Me? I Mean It!) Going to Move* (Focus on practicing reading with a range of emotions.) Pigeon series by Mo Willems: *Don't Let the Pigeon Drive the Bus!, Don't Let the Pigeon Stay Up Late!, The Pigeon Finds a Hot Dog!, The Pigeon Has Feelings, Too!, The Pigeon Needs a Bath!, The Pigeon Wants a Puppy!* *Yo! Yes?* and *Ring! Yo?* by Chris Raschka
Grades	K–1
Length of Activity	10–30 minutes
Location	school or home
Extension Idea	• Echo-read the stories with students, asking them to match your voice as you read them together.

1.D Developing Fluency Through Song

Songs are perfect for developing early fluency in children because melody is a form of prosody, or expression. Furthermore, when children sing songs and, at the same time, have their eyes on the printed lyrics, they are well on their way to developing all aspects of fluency. Since

the rhythm, rhyme, and melodies in songs make them easy to learn and remember, children will actually begin to recognize and decode lyrics.

Introduce students to a song or two every week. Project the lyrics so children can easily see them. Sing the song to the children until they grasp the melody and the words. (You can find instrumental versions of children's songs on YouTube.) Then, over the course of several days, sing the song with students in various ways (whole class, small group, individually, etc.). Be sure to draw children's attention to each word in the song by pointing to it. And enjoy!

Materials Needed	Copy of a childhood song to project for the class and distribute to each student (pp. 26–30): "London Bridge," "Polly Wolly Doodle," "Home on the Range," "My Bonnie Lies Over the Ocean," "I've Been Working on the Railroad." (Complete lyrics can be found at www.kididdles.com/lyrics/allsongs.html)
Grades	K–3
Length of Activity	15 minutes
Location	school or home
Extension Idea	• Once students have mastered a song, work with them to select individual words from the song and put them on a word wall. Then, in addition to singing the song, have students read the words on the wall to develop word recognition automaticity. • Swap out words in a familiar song, or find parodies of it, to keep it fresh for students and to keep them on their toes when singing it. Author Alan Katz is an expert at creating parodies of children's songs. Here are few of his best-loved books: *I'm Still Here in the Bathtub, Take Me Out of the Bathtub, Where Did They Hide My Presents?*

Fluency Skills Practiced

E
Expression

A
Automatic Word Recognition

R
Rhythm and Phrasing

S
Smoothness

London Bridge

London Bridge is falling down,
Falling down, falling down.
London Bridge is falling down,
My fair lady!

Build it up with iron bars,
Iron bars, iron bars.
Build it up with iron bars,
My fair lady!

Iron bars will bend and break,
Bend and break, bend and break.
Iron bars will bend and break,
My fair lady!

Polly Wolly Doodle

Oh, I went down South

For to see my Sal

Sing Polly wolly doodle all the day.

My Sal, she is

A spunky gal

Sing Polly wolly doodle all the day.

Fare thee well,

Fare thee well,

Fare thee well my fairy fay.

For I'm going to Louisiana

For to see my Susyanna

Sing Polly wolly doodle all the day.

Home on the Range

Oh, give me a home where the buffalo roam
And the deer and the antelope play.
Where seldom is heard a discouraging word
And the skies are not cloudy all day.

Home, home on the range
Where the deer and the antelope play.
Where seldom is heard a discouraging word
And the skies are not cloudy all day.

My Bonnie Lies Over the Ocean

My Bonnie lies over the ocean
My Bonnie lies over the sea
My Bonnie lies over the ocean
Oh bring back my Bonnie to me.

Bring back, bring back
Bring back my Bonnie to me, to me.
Bring back, bring back
Bring back my Bonnie to me.

The winds will blow over the ocean
The winds will blow over the sea
The winds will blow over the ocean
To bring back my Bonnie to me.

Bring back, bring back
Bring back my Bonnie to me, to me.
Bring back, bring back
Bring back my Bonnie to me.

Bring back, bring back
Oh, bring back my Bonnie to me.

I've Been Working on the Railroad

I've been working on the railroad
All the live-long day.
I've been working on the railroad
Just to pass the time away.
Can't you hear the whistle blowing,
Rise up so early in the morn;
Can't you hear the captain shouting,
"Dinah, blow your horn!"

Dinah, won't you blow,
Dinah, won't you blow,
Dinah, won't you blow your horn?
Dinah, won't you blow,
Dinah, won't you blow,
Dinah, won't you blow your horn?

Someone's in the kitchen with Dinah
Someone's in the kitchen I know
Someone's in the kitchen with Dinah
Strumming on the old banjo!

Singin' fee, fie, fiddly-i-o
Fee, fie, fiddly-i-o-o-o-o
Fee, fie, fiddly-i-o
Strumming on the old banjo.

1.E Developing Fluency Through Rhyme and Poetry

Rhymes and poems for children are excellent and joyful choices for developing early fluency. When children recite the words to poems and, at the same time, have their eyes on the printed words in the poem, they are well on their way to developing all aspects of fluency. Since the rhythm and rhyme in poems make them easy to learn and remember, children will actually begin to recognize and decode the poem's words.

Introduce students to a poem or two every week. Project the poem so that the children can easily see the words. Read the poem to the children with good (even exaggerated) expression until they have memorized it. Then, over the course of several days, recite the poem with students in various ways (whole class, small group, individually, alternate lines, etc.). Be sure to draw children's attention to each word as they are read by pointing to it.

Materials Needed	Copy of a childhood rhyme or poem to project for the class and distribute to each student (pp. 32–36): "Diddle, Diddle Dumpling," "Hickory, Dickory Dock," "Baa, Baa, Black Sheep," "To Market, to Market," "B-I-N-G-O."
Grades	K–5
Length of Activity	15–20 minutes
Location	school or home
Extension Ideas	• Once students have mastered a poem, work with them to select individual words from it and put them on a word wall. Then, in addition to reciting the poem, have students read the words on the wall to develop word recognition automaticity. • Once the poem is mastered, create a parody and continue reading with your students. • Swap out words in a familiar poem, or find parodies of it, to keep it fresh for students and to keep them on their toes when reciting it. A great source for children's rhymes is www.nurseryrhymes.org. Some of our favorite poets for children of all ages include: Brod Bagert (www.brodbagert.org), Bruce Lansky (gigglepoetry.com), David Harrison (www.davidlharrison.com), Jack Prelutsky (www.jackprelutsky.com), Kenn Nesbitt (www.poetry4kids.com), Robert Pottle (www.robertpottle.com/poems)

Fluency Skills Practiced

E

Expression

A

Automatic Word Recognition

R

Rhythm and Phrasing

S

Smoothness

Diddle, Diddle Dumpling

Diddle, diddle dumpling,
My son, John,
Went to bed
With his stockings on;
One shoe off
And one shoe on,
Diddle, diddle dumpling,
My son, John.

Extension

Diddle, diddle dumpling,
My girl, Mag,
Had a dog
And his name was Tag;
Tag had a tail
That would wiggle and wag,
Diddle, diddle dumpling,
My girl, Mag.

Hickory Dickory Dock

Hickory, dickory, dock
The mouse ran up the clock.
The clock struck one
The mouse ran down
Hickory, dickory, dock.

Extension

Hickory, dickory, dock
The robin flew up the clock.
The clock struck two
The birdy flew
Hickory, dickory, dock.

Hickory, dickory, dox.
The mouse ran into a box.
A dog named Rover
Tipped the box over.
Hickory, dickory, dox.

Baa, Baa, Black Sheep

Baa, baa, black sheep
Have you any wool?
Yes sir, yes sir
Three bags full.
One for my master
And one for the dame
One for the little boy
Who lives down the lane.

Baa, baa, black sheep
Have you any wool?
Yes sir, yes sir
Three bags full.

To Market, to Market

To market, to market, to buy a fat pig,
Home again, home again, jiggety-jig.

To market, to market, to buy a fat hog,
Home again, home again, jiggety-jog.

To market, to market, to buy a plum bun,
Home again, home again, market
is done.

B-I-N-G-O

There was a farmer who had a dog,
And Bingo was his name-o.
B-I-N-G-O
B-I-N-G-O
B-I-N-G-O
And Bingo was his name-o.

There was a farmer who had a dog,
And Bingo was his name-o.
B-I-N-G-O
B-I-N-G-O
B-I-N-G-O
And Bingo was his name-o.

There was a farmer who had a dog,
And Bingo was his name-o.
B-I-N-G-O
B-I-N-G-O
B-I-N-G-O
And Bingo was his name-o.

1.F Patterned Picture Book Readings

Look for picture books with predictable patterns and read them aloud as students follow along, repeating phrases with you when cued. Although they may not yet be reading conventionally, students can start the process by practicing phrasing and expression, before being able to decode the words, by reading with you this way.

Materials Needed	Picture books such as: • *Again!* by John Prater • *Bear Snores On* by Karma Wilson • *Brown Bear, Brown Bear, What Do You See?* by Bill Martin • *Click, Clack, Moo: Cows That Type* by Doreen Cronin • *Dooby, Dooby, Moo* by Doreen Cronin • *Giggle, Giggle, Quack* by Doreen Cronin • *Goodnight Moon* by Margaret Wise Brown • *I Went Walking* by Sue Williams • If You Give … book series by Laura Joffe Numeroff • *Knock, Knock* by Sophie Blackall • *Owl Babies* by Martin Waddell • There Was an Old Lady Who Swallowed a … series by Lucille Colandro • *Thump, Quack, Moo* by Doreen Cronin
Grades	K–1
Length of Activity	10–30 minutes
Location	school or home

CHAPTER 2

Teach Expressive
Fluency: It's All
in How You
Say It!

Videos and
downloadables
are available at
**Scholastic.com/
FluencyResources.**

CHAPTER 2

Teach Expressive Fluency: It's All in How You Say It!

"The longer I live, the more I see there's something about reciting rhythmical words aloud—it's almost biological—it has the ability to comfort and enliven human beings."

—Robert Pinsky

Think of people you consider "fluent" speakers—actors or politicians, perhaps. What is it that makes those people fluent? Is it because they speak at a fast pace? Or perhaps just the opposite—they speak at a slow and deliberate pace. Maybe it's the way they hold themselves when speaking—good posture, eye contact, a confident air about them. Actually, all these things work together to create fluent speech. Fluent speakers emphasize certain words and phrases, exaggerate pauses, change their volume from loud to soft and back again, and raise and lower their pitch and tone. Fluency in speaking is complex.

Why do fluent speakers use their voice in these ways? Why not just say the words they wish to say in a manner that might be described as staccato and atonal, and at a neutral pace? Because their fluency enhances the meaning they wish to convey. Fluent, expressive speech is more compelling to listen to than less fluent speech, and is easier to understand than less fluent speech. In essence, fluent speech is more engaging for and increases comprehension of the listener.

Fluent speech and fluent reading are analogous. Like fluent speakers, fluent readers think about words and phrases to emphasize and places to pause, increase volume, change pitch and tone. Why? To make the reading more engaging and meaningful. The big difference between fluent speech and fluent reading is that the audience for the fluent reader is usually the reader him- or herself.

Research has demonstrated time and again that readers who read orally with fluency tend to comprehend more deeply when reading, whether silently or orally (Rasinski, Reutzel, Chard, & Linan-Thompson, 2011). Moreover, less fluent readers (e.g., excessively slow, staccato, unconfident, atonal) experience more difficulty comprehending, even if they read with excellent word recognition. Moreover, many students across the grade levels do not read with what we might call good fluency or expression. This problem, we think, is due to the fact that fluent and expressive oral reading is seldom taught. With the great emphasis on silent reading, little attention is given to fluent oral reading as a way to understand and express the meaning of a passage.

This book attempts to remedy that situation. In this chapter, you will find several activities that allow students to "play" with their voices in order to affect meaning. The intent of these activities is to put expressive speaking and reading on the instructional radar screen. As students engage in these activities, you will have the opportunity to discuss how their voices can affect meaning. Of course, the discussion should lead to reading text with good oral expression, and, when reading silently, to read in a way that the reader hears an internal voice. We hope you will use the activities as a jumping-off point for making expressive speech and reading a regular part of your instruction.

Strategies

**Fluency Skills
Practiced**

E

Expression

A

Automatic
Word Recognition

R

Rhythm
and Phrasing

S

Smoothness

2.A **Emphasizing Words**

She didn't ask Dad to go to the mall.

She didn't ask Dad to go to the mall.

Someone else asked dad.

She **didn't** ask Dad to go to the mall.

Someone thought she did, but she's saying she didn't.

She didn't **ask** Dad to go to the mall.

It may have not been a question to dad, but more of a demand.

She didn't ask **Dad** to go to the mall.

Students read individual sentences aloud, emphasizing the boldfaced word. Then they explain how emphasizing that word impacts the sentence's meaning. Students may need you to demonstrate the strategy before trying it themselves. This strategy works well when it is done with partners so that students can read aloud and debate the meaning of the sentences.

Materials Needed	Copy of an Emphasizing Words page for each student (pp. 41–46)
Grades	2–8 (change complexity of sentence structure depending on grade level)
Length of Activity	10 minutes
Location	school or home
Extension Ideas	• Create your own sentences related to content you are teaching. For example, when studying the solar system, create a sentence with a content-area word in it such as: *Jenny looked at the red moon.* Keep the sentences simple enough that students can find different ways to emphasize words. • When creating your own sentences, be aware that not every word needs to be emphasized. Just a few key words can do the trick.

The Mall

> **Directions:** Emphasizing certain words in a sentence can change the meaning. Read each sentence aloud, emphasizing the boldfaced word, and explain how the meaning changes.

She didn't ask Dad to go to the mall.

She didn't ask Dad to go to the mall.

She **didn't** ask Dad to go to the mall.

She didn't **ask** Dad to go to the mall.

She didn't ask **Dad** to go to the mall.

She didn't ask Dad to go to the **mall.**

After School

> **Directions:** Emphasizing certain words in a sentence can change the meaning. Read each sentence aloud, emphasizing the boldfaced word, and explain how the meaning changes.

Olivia wanted to practice the piano after school.

Olivia wanted to practice the piano after school.

Olivia **wanted** to practice the piano after school.

Olivia wanted to **practice** the piano after school.

Olivia wanted to practice the **piano** after school.

Olivia wanted to practice the piano after **school.**

Tuesday Night

Directions: Emphasizing certain words in a sentence can change the meaning. Read each sentence aloud, emphasizing the boldfaced word, and explain how the meaning changes.

Julio wanted to stargaze on Tuesday night.

Julio wanted to stargaze on Tuesday night.

Julio **wanted** to stargaze on Tuesday night.

Julio wanted to **stargaze** on Tuesday night.

Julio wanted to stargaze on **Tuesday** night.

Julio wanted to stargaze on Tuesday **night.**

Chocolate Chip Cookies

Directions: Emphasizing certain words in a sentence can change the meaning. Read each sentence aloud, emphasizing the boldfaced word, and explain how the meaning changes.

Jill ate Mom's chocolate chip cookies.

Jill ate Mom's chocolate chip cookies.

Jill **ate** Mom's chocolate chip cookies.

Jill ate **Mom's** chocolate chip cookies.

Jill ate Mom's **chocolate chip** cookies.

Jill ate Mom's chocolate chip **cookies.**

Video Games

Directions: Emphasizing certain words in a sentence can change the meaning. Read each sentence aloud, emphasizing the boldfaced word, and explain how the meaning changes.

Lydia loved her video games.

Lydia loved her video games.

Lydia **loved** her video games.

Lydia loved **her** video games.

Lydia loved her **video** games.

Lydia loved her video **games.**

Basketball

Directions: Emphasizing certain words in a sentence can change the meaning. Read each sentence aloud, emphasizing the boldfaced word, and explain how the meaning changes.

Tom borrowed my new basketball.

Tom borrowed my new basketball.

Tom **borrowed** my new basketball.

Tom borrowed **my** new basketball.

Tom borrowed my **new** basketball.

Tom borrowed my new **basketball.**

2.B **Connotation in Context**

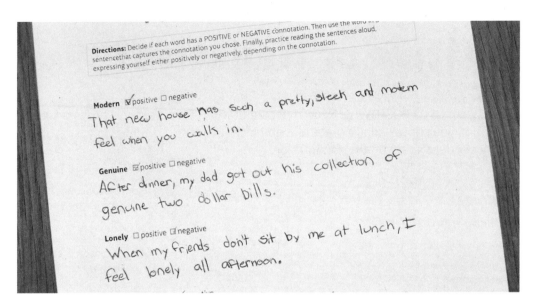

Directions: Decide if each word has a POSITIVE or NEGATIVE connotation. Then use the word in a sentence that captures the connotation you chose. Finally, practice reading the sentences aloud, expressing yourself either positively or negatively, depending on the connotation.

Modern ☑ positive ☐ negative
That new house has such a pretty, sleek and modern feel when you walks in.

Genuine ☑ positive ☐ negative
After dinner, my dad got out his collection of genuine two dollar bills.

Lonely ☐ positive ☑ negative
When my friends don't sit by me at lunch, I feel lonely all afternoon.

Students are given a series of words and are asked to decide whether each one has a positive connotation or a negative connotation. Then they use the word in a sentence that captures the connotation they chose using context clues. You may need to model this to show that the same word can have a different connotation depending on the context used. When they've finished writing their sentences, students practice reading them aloud, expressing themselves either positively or negatively depending on the connotation.

Materials Needed	Copy of a Connotation in Context page for each student (pp. 48–51) Pencil for each student
Grades	4–8
Length of Activity	10 minutes
Location	school or home
Extension Idea	• Have students learn the subtleties of word connotations by giving them a word and its synonyms and asking them to order the words on a continuum, such as words that mean *happy*, least to greatest: *happy, cheerful, joyful, ecstatic.* This helps students think about the nuances of words.

Fluency Skills Practiced

E
Expression

☑

A
Automatic
Word Recognition

☑

R
Rhythm
and Phrasing

☑

S
Smoothness

☑

Name: _____ Date: _____

Positive or Negative?

Directions: Decide if each word has a POSITIVE or NEGATIVE connotation. Then use the word in a sentence that captures the connotation you chose. Finally, practice reading the sentences aloud, expressing yourself either positively or negatively, depending on the connotation.

modern ☐ positive ☐ negative

_____

_____

genuine ☐ positive ☐ negative

_____

_____

lonely ☐ positive ☐ negative

_____

_____

strong ☐ positive ☐ negative

_____

_____

rough ☐ positive ☐ negative

_____

_____

Name: _____ Date: _____

Positive or Negative?

Directions: Decide if each word has a POSITIVE or NEGATIVE connotation. Then use the word in a sentence that captures the connotation you chose. Finally, practice reading the sentences aloud, expressing yourself either positively or negatively, depending on the connotation.

mushy ☐ positive ☐ negative

_____

_____

chatty ☐ positive ☐ negative

_____

_____

weird ☐ positive ☐ negative

_____

_____

strong-willed ☐ positive ☐ negative

_____

_____

wild ☐ positive ☐ negative

_____

_____

Name: _____   Date: _____

Positive or Negative?

Directions: Decide if each word has a POSITIVE or NEGATIVE connotation. Then use the word in a sentence that captures the connotation you chose. Finally, practice reading the sentences aloud, expressing yourself either positively or negatively, depending on the connotation.

dull ☐ positive ☐ negative

_____

_____

pushy ☐ positive ☐ negative

_____

_____

aggressive ☐ positive ☐ negative

_____

_____

dynamic ☐ positive ☐ negative

_____

_____

mousey ☐ positive ☐ negative

_____

_____

Name: _____   Date: _____

Positive or Negative?

Directions: Decide if each word has a POSITIVE or NEGATIVE connotation. Then use the word in a sentence that captures the connotation you chose. Finally, practice reading the sentences aloud, expressing yourself either positively or negatively, depending on the connotation.

thrifty ☐ positive ☐ negative

_____

_____

classic ☐ positive ☐ negative

_____

_____

bumpy ☐ positive ☐ negative

_____

_____

bulky ☐ positive ☐ negative

_____

_____

challenge ☐ positive ☐ negative

_____

_____

**Fluency Skills
Practiced**

E

Expression

☑

A

Automatic
Word Recognition

☐

R

Rhythm
and Phrasing

☑

S

Smoothness

☐

2.C Match That Expression

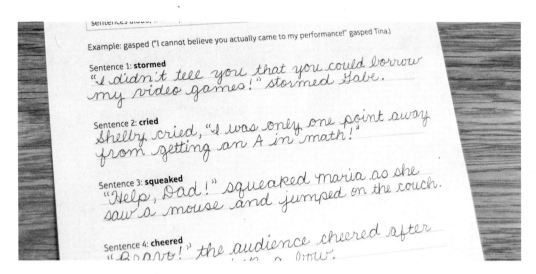

Students are given synonyms for the word *said* and are asked to write sentences containing the word as a descriptor for how the quoted words were said. Each sentence should include a quotation and enough context clues for the listener to understand the meaning of the synonym. Students then read their sentences aloud with expression. This activity helps students avoid overusing *said* in writing, as well as build their fluency skills as they practice reading aloud with expression.

Materials Needed	Copy of a Match That Expression page for each student (pp. 53–57) Pencil for each student
Grades	2–8 (levels increase in complexity of vocabulary)
Length of Activity	10 minutes
Location	school
Extension Ideas	• Create your own sentences that capture the level of vocabulary you're teaching. For example, with younger students, words such as *bragged* or *shouted* could be used, and with older students, words such as *uttered* or *conceded*. • Have a student read the sentence aloud, leaving out the target word, while the other students guess the missing word based on context clues and the expression used by the reader. • Give feedback in small groups or to partners. • When reading aloud with students, point out how authors use words other than *said*.

Name: _____   Date: _____

Synonyms for *Said*

Directions: The words below are synonyms for *said*. Write a sentence that contains each word and matches the feeling of the word (see example). Then, practice reading the sentences aloud, with expression.

Example: **gasped** ("I cannot believe you actually came to my performance!" gasped Tina.)

Sentence 1: **stormed**

_____

_____

Sentence 2: **cried**

_____

_____

Sentence 3: **squeaked**

_____

_____

Sentence 4: **cheered**

_____

_____

Sentence 5: **screeched**

_____

_____

Sentence 6: **joked**

_____

_____

Name: _____   Date: _____

Synonyms for *Said*

Directions: The words below are synonyms for *said*. Write a sentence that contains each word and matches the feeling of the word (see example). Then, practice reading the sentences aloud, with expression.

Example: **gasped** ("I cannot believe you actually came to my performance!" gasped Tina.)

Sentence 1: **reminded**

_____

_____

Sentence 2: **snapped**

_____

_____

Sentence 3: **argued**

_____

_____

Sentence 4: **blurted**

_____

_____

Sentence 5: **suggested**

_____

_____

Sentence 6: **begged**

_____

_____

Name: _____   Date: _____

Synonyms for *Said*

Directions: The words below are synonyms for *said*. Write a sentence that contains each word and matches the feeling of the word (see example). Then, practice reading the sentences aloud, with expression.

Example: **gasped** ("I cannot believe you actually came to my performance!" gasped Tina.)

Sentence 1: **ordered**

_____

_____

Sentence 2: **nagged**

_____

_____

Sentence 3: **scolded**

_____

_____

Sentence 4: **barked**

_____

_____

Sentence 5: **chuckled**

_____

_____

Sentence 6: **debated**

_____

_____

Name: _____   Date: _____

Synonyms for *Said*

Directions: The words below are synonyms for *said*. Write a sentence that contains each word and matches the feeling of the word (see example). Then, practice reading the sentences aloud, with expression.

Example: **gasped** ("I cannot believe you actually came to my performance!" gasped Tina.)

Sentence 1: **judged**

_____

_____

Sentence 2: **advised**

_____

_____

Sentence 3: **ranted**

_____

_____

Sentence 4: **interrogated**

_____

_____

Sentence 5: **remarked**

_____

_____

Sentence 6: **mumbled**

_____

_____

Name: _____   Date: _____

Synonyms for *Said*

Directions: The words below are synonyms for *said*. Write a sentence that contains each word and matches the feeling of the word (see example). Then, practice reading the sentences aloud, with expression.

Example: **gasped** ("I cannot believe you actually came to my performance!" gasped Tina.)

Sentence 1: **admonished**

_____

_____

Sentence 2: **disclosed**

_____

_____

Sentence 3: **rejoiced**

_____

_____

Sentence 4: **insinuated**

_____

_____

Sentence 5: **bantered**

_____

_____

Sentence 6: **affirmed**

_____

_____

**Fluency Skills
Practiced**

E

Expression

A

Automatic
Word Recognition

R

Rhythm
and Phrasing

S

Smoothness

2.D **Phrasing Nonsense**

Students practice using punctuation to read with expression. They start by inserting punctuation marks into "nonsense" passages (e.g., letters only, numbers only, and "blah, blah, blah" only). Then they practice reading their passage to a partner. For example, a student could write "A, B, C! D E." Then, as they read, they would pause after each comma and elevate their voice at the exclamation point. From there, they would pause after the period before starting to read the next "sentence."

Materials Needed	Copy of a Phrasing Nonsense page for each student (pp. 59–61) Pencil for each student
Grades	2–8
Length of Activity	10–15 minutes
Location	school or home
Extension Ideas	• Consider carrying out this activity on the whiteboard, with no copies distributed. The passages could then be read chorally, exaggerating points where punctuation has been added. • Use the same text repeatedly, each time marking it with different punctuation. • To assess students, copy a passage that has been pre-marked with punctuation and have students read it individually to see if they are pausing briefly for commas, pausing longer for periods, showing excitement for exclamation points, ending in an "up" sound for questions, and so forth. • Have each student practice reading with a partner, with each partner guessing the punctuation that was added. This will help readers and listeners pay attention when reading aloud.

Name: _____   Date: _____

The Alphabet

Directions: Insert punctuation marks into the passage below. Then read the passage with expression, focusing on the punctuation you inserted.

Punctuation marks to use:

periods	commas	exclamation points	question marks	quotation marks	colon
.	,	!	?	" "	:

A B C D E

F G H I J K

L M N O P

Q R S T U

V W X Y Z

Name: _____   Date: _____

Numbers

Directions: Insert punctuation marks into the passage below. Then read the passage with expression, focusing on the punctuation you inserted.

Punctuation marks to use:

periods	commas	exclamation points	question marks	quotation marks	colon
.	,	!	?	" "	:

1 2 3 4 5

6 7 8 9 10

11 12 13 14 15

16 17 18 19 20

Name: _____   Date: _____

Blah Blah Blah

Directions: Insert punctuation marks into the passage below. Then read the passage with expression, focusing on the punctuation you inserted.

Punctuation marks to use:

periods	commas	exclamation points	question marks	quotation marks	colon
.	,	!	?	" "	:

Blah   blah   blah   blah

blah   blah   blah   blah

blah   blah   blah   blah

blah   blah   blah   blah

**Fluency Skills
Practiced**

E

Expression

A

Automatic
Word Recognition

R

Rhythm
and Phrasing

S

Smoothness

2.E **Text Phrasing**

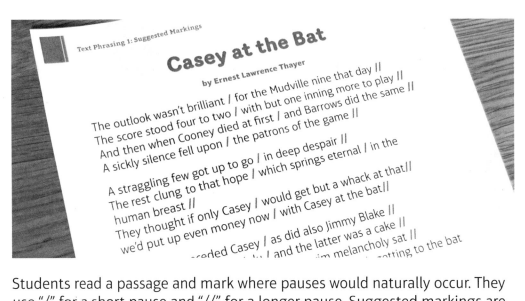

Text Phrasing 1: Suggested Markings

Casey at the Bat

by Ernest Lawrence Thayer

The outlook wasn't brilliant / for the Mudville nine that day //
The score stood four to two / with but one inning more to play //
And then when Cooney died at first / and Barrows did the same //
A sickly silence fell upon / the patrons of the game //

A straggling few got up to go / in deep despair //
The rest clung to that hope / which springs eternal / in the
human breast //
They thought if only Casey / would get but a whack at that//
we'd put up even money now / with Casey at the bat//

...eded Casey / as did also Jimmy Blake //
...... / and the latter was a cake //
.... melancholy sat //
...tting to the bat

Students read a passage and mark where pauses would naturally occur. They use "/" for a short pause and "//" for a longer pause. Suggested markings are included after each passage.

Materials Needed	Copy of a Text Phrasing page for each student (pp. 63–72) Pencil for each student
Grades	2–8 (levels increase in complexity of vocabulary)
Length of Activity	10–20 minutes
Location	school or home
Extension Ideas	• Have students work with partners to determine where the phrase boundaries should go. Encourage them to read the passage aloud and discuss. • Give students the "suggested markings" page to practice pausing as they read. Tell them there isn't only one right way to mark up these passages but that these are suggestions.

Name: _____   Date: _____

> **Directions:** Mark the text to show where short pauses and long pauses should go when reading it aloud. / = short pause, // = long pause

Casey at the Bat

(excerpt)

by Ernest Lawrence Thayer

The outlook wasn't brilliant for the Mudville nine that day
The score stood four to two with but one inning more to play
And then when Cooney died at first and Barrows did the same
A sickly silence fell upon the patrons of the game

A straggling few got up to go in deep despair The rest
clung to that hope which springs eternal in the human breast
They thought if only Casey could get but a whack at that
We'd put up even money now with Casey at the bat

But Flynn preceded Casey as did also Jimmy Blake
And the former was a lulu and the latter was a cake
So upon that stricken multitude grim melancholy sat
For there seemed but little chance of Casey's getting to the bat

Casey at the Bat

(excerpt)

by Ernest Lawrence Thayer

The outlook wasn't brilliant **/** for the Mudville nine that day **//**
The score stood four to two **/** with but one inning more to play **//**
And then when Cooney died at first **/** and Barrows did the same **//**
A sickly silence fell upon **/** the patrons of the game **//**

A straggling few got up to go **/** in deep despair **//**
The rest clung to that hope **/** which springs eternal **/** in the
human breast **//**
They thought if only Casey **/** would get but a whack at that**//**
we'd put up even money now **/** with Casey at the bat**//**

But Flynn preceded Casey **/** as did also Jimmy Blake **//**
And the former was a lulu **/** and the latter was a cake **//**
So upon that stricken multitude **/** grim melancholy sat **//**
For there seemed but little chance **/** of Casey's getting to the bat

Name: _____   Date: _____

> **Directions:** Mark the text to show where short pauses and long pauses should go when reading it aloud. / = short pause, // = long pause

The Gettysburg Address

by Abraham Lincoln

Four score and seven years ago our fathers brought forth on this continent a new nation conceived in Liberty and dedicated to the proposition that all men are created equal

Now we are engaged in a great civil war testing whether that nation or any nation so conceived and so dedicated can long endure We are met on a great battle-field of that war We have come to dedicate a portion of that field as a final resting place for those who here gave their lives that that nation might live It is altogether fitting and proper that we should do this

But in a larger sense we cannot dedicate we cannot consecrate we cannot hallow this ground The brave men living and dead who struggled here have consecrated it far above our poor power to add or detract The world will little note nor long remember what we say here but it can never forget what they did here It is for us the living rather to be dedicated here to the unfinished work which they who fought here have thus far so nobly advanced It is rather for us to be here dedicated to the great task remaining before us that from these honored dead we take increased devotion to that cause for which they gave the last full measure of devotion that we here highly resolve that these dead shall not have died in vain that this nation under God shall have a new birth of freedom and that government of the people by the people for the people shall not perish from the earth

The Gettysburg Address

by Abraham Lincoln

Four score and seven years ago / our fathers brought forth / on this continent / a new nation / conceived in Liberty / and dedicated to the proposition / that all men are created equal//

Now we are engaged in a great civil war / testing whether that nation / or any nation so conceived / and so dedicated / can long endure // We are met on a great battlefield of that war // We have come to dedicate a portion of that field / as a final resting place / for those / who here gave their lives / that that nation might live // It is altogether fitting and proper / that we should do this //

But / in a larger sense / we cannot dedicate / we cannot consecrate / we cannot hallow this ground // The brave men / living and dead / who struggled here / have consecrated it far above our poor power to add or detract // The world will little note nor long remember what we say here // but it can never forget / what they did here // It is for us the living / rather to be dedicated here / to the unfinished work / which they who fought here / have thus far so nobly advanced // It is rather for us / to be here dedicated / to the great task remaining before us // that from these honored dead / we take increased devotion / to that cause / for which they gave the last full measure of devotion // that we here highly resolve / that these dead shall not have died in vain / that this nation / under God / shall have a new birth of freedom // and that government of the people / by the people / for the people / shall not perish from the earth

Name: _____ Date: _____

> **Directions:** Mark the text to show where short pauses and long pauses should go when reading it aloud. / = short pause, // = long pause

Inaugural Address

(excerpt)

by John F. Kennedy

In the long history of the world only a few generations have been granted the role of defending freedom in its hour of maximum danger I do not shrink from this responsibility I welcome it I do not believe that any of us would exchange places with any other people or any other generation The energy the faith the devotion which we bring to this endeavor will light our country and all who serve it And the glow from that fire can truly light the world

And so my fellow Americans ask not what your country can do for you ask what you can do for your country

My fellow citizens of the world ask not what America will do for you but what together we can do for the freedom of man

Finally whether you are citizens of America or citizens of the world ask of us here the same high standards of strength and sacrifice which we ask of you With a good conscience our only sure reward with history the final judge of our deeds let us go forth to lead the land we love asking His blessing and His help but knowing that here on earth God's work must truly be our own

Inaugural Address

(excerpt)

by John F. Kennedy

In the long history of the world / only a few generations have been granted the role of defending freedom / in its hour of maximum danger // I do not shrink from this responsibility / I welcome it // I do not believe / that any of us would exchange places / with any other people / or any other generation // The energy / the faith / the devotion which we bring to this endeavor / will light our country / and all who serve it // And the glow from that fire / can truly light the world //

And so my fellow Americans / ask not what your country can do for you // ask what you can do for your country //

My fellow citizens of the world / ask not what America will do for you // but what together we can do for the freedom of man//

Finally / whether you are citizens of America / or citizens of the world / ask of us here / the same high standards of strength and sacrifice / which we ask of you // With a good conscience / our only sure reward with history the final judge of our deeds / let us go forth to lead the land we love / asking His blessing and His help / but knowing that here on earth / God's work must truly be our own

Name: _____   Date: _____

> **Directions:** Mark the text to show where short pauses and long pauses should go when reading it aloud. / = short pause, // = long pause

Paul Revere's Ride

(excerpt)

by Henry Wadsworth Longfellow

Listen my children and you shall hear
Of the midnight ride of Paul Revere
On the eighteenth of April in Seventy-Five
Hardly a man is now alive
Who remembers that famous day and year

He said to his friend "If the British march
By land or sea from the town to-night
Hang a lantern aloft in the belfry arch
Of the North Church tower as a signal light
One if by land and two if by sea
And I on the opposite shore will be
Ready to ride and spread the alarm
Through every Middlesex village and farm
For the country folk to be up and to arm"

Paul Revere's Ride

(excerpt)

by Henry Wadsworth Longfellow

Listen my children **/** and you shall hear **/**
Of the midnight ride **/** of Paul Revere **//**
On the eighteenth of April **/** in Seventy-Five **/**
Hardly a man **/** is now alive **/**
Who remembers **/** that famous day and year **//**

He said to his friend **/** "If the British march **/**
By land or sea **/** from the town tonight **/**
Hang a lantern aloft **/** in the belfry arch **/**
Of the North Church tower **/** as a signal light **/**
One if by land **/** and two if by sea **//**
And I **/** on the opposite shore **/** will be **/**
Ready to ride **/** and spread the alarm **/**
Through every Middlesex village and farm **/**
For the country folk **/** to be up **/** and to arm"

Name: _____   Date: _____

> **Directions:** Mark the text to show where short pauses and long pauses should go when reading it aloud. / = short pause, // = long pause

Hansel and Gretel

(excerpt)

by Jacob and Wilhelm Grimm

Next to a great forest there lived a poor woodcutter with his wife and his two children The boy's name was Hansel and the girl's name was Gretel He had but little to eat and once when a great famine came to the land he could no longer provide even their daily bread

One evening as he was lying in bed worrying about his problems he sighed and said to his wife "What is to become of us? How can we feed our children when we have nothing for ourselves?"

"Man do you know what?" answered the woman "Early tomorrow morning we will take the two children out into the thickest part of the woods make a fire for them and give each of them a little piece of bread then leave them by themselves and go off to our work They will not find their way back home and we will be rid of them"

"No woman" said the man "I will not do that How could I bring myself to abandon my own children alone in the woods? Wild animals would soon come and tear them to pieces"

"Oh you fool" she said "then all four of us will starve All you can do is to plane the boards for our coffins" And she gave him no peace until he agreed

"But I do feel sorry for the poor children" said the man

Hansel and Gretel

(excerpt)

by Jacob and Wilhelm Grimm

Next to a great forest / there lived a poor woodcutter / with his wife / and his two children // The boy's name was Hansel / and the girl's name was Gretel // He had but little to eat / and once / when a great famine came to the land / he could no longer provide / even their daily bread//

One evening / as he was lying in bed / worrying about his problems / he sighed and said to his wife / "What is to become of us? / How can we feed our children / when we have nothing for ourselves?"//

"Man / do you know what?" / answered the woman // "Early tomorrow morning / we will take the two children out / into the thickest part of the woods / make a fire for them / and give each of them a little piece of bread / then leave them by themselves / and go off to our work // They will not find their way back home / and we will be rid of them"//

"No / woman"/ said the man // "I will not do that // How could I bring myself / to abandon my own children / alone in the woods?// Wild animals would soon come / and tear them to pieces"//

"Oh / you fool"/ she said / "then all four of us will starve // All you can do / is to plane the boards / for our coffins" // And she gave him no peace / until he agreed //

"But I do feel sorry / for the poor children"/ said the man

2.F **Marking Up Expression**

Jennifer couldn't believe her luck! She had never won anything in her life, and she'd just won the drawing contest at school. No doubt she worked hard to earn it, spending hours on her drawing of a new school mascot, but she was elated that she had actually won! Who would have thought? Now she just had to decide how to spend her winning money: 100 dollars! She knew she'd share it with her best friends Katie, Jackie, and Sarah. She couldn't wait to tell them the good news and she ran towards the playground.

Students read a text and then mark it to remind themselves when and how to read it aloud with expression. Then they practice reading the marked-up text aloud, paying special attention to their notes.

Materials Needed	Copy of the Marking Chart for each student (p. 74) Copy of a Marking Up Expression page for each student (pp. 75–81) Pencil for each student
Grades	4–8
Length of Activity	10 minutes
Location	school or home
Extension Idea	• Use a common text read in class (literature study book, literature circle book, etc.) and copy a short passage or page, then have students mark with expression and practice reading aloud.

Fluency Skills Practiced

E

Expression

A

Automatic Word Recognition

R

Rhythm and Phrasing

S

Smoothness

Marking Chart

	Text Signal	Marking	What to Do While Reading
,	Comma	/	pause briefly
.	Period	//	pause
?	Question Mark	↶	raise your tone at the end of the line
!	Exclamation Point	✳	read with excitement or other emotion
" ___ "	Quotation Marks	☺ ☹ 😐	read in the voice of whoever is speaking
...	Ellipsis	• • •	trail off, as if there is more to the passage
		underline to highlight points you want to emphasize	alter your voice to emphasize the point
		↓	slow down
		↑	speed up

Name: _____   Date: _____

Drawing Contest

Directions: Using the Marking Chart as a reference, mark the text below to remind yourself when and how to read it aloud with expression. Then practice reading it aloud, paying special attention to your notes.

Jennifer couldn't believe her luck! She had never won anything in her life, and she'd just won the drawing contest at school. No doubt she worked hard to earn it, spending hours on her drawing of a new school mascot, but she was elated that she had actually won! Who would have thought? Now she just had to decide how to spend her winning money: 100 dollars! She knew she'd share it with her best friends Katie, Jackie, and Sarah. She couldn't wait to tell them the good news, and she ran towards the playground.

Name: _____ Date: _____

Spooky House

> **Directions:** Using the Marking Chart as a reference, mark the text below to remind yourself when and how to read it aloud with expression. Then practice reading it aloud, paying special attention to your notes.

Slowly, Casey opened the door to the empty house. None of his friends had ever before been brave enough to actually go in the spooky house in the neighborhood, and now, here he was, sun going down, going in all by himself. He was surprised to find the door unlocked, and his friends were cheering him on from the yard, but that didn't help to calm his nerves. As soon as Casey entered, there was a strong and horrible smell, and he saw something dart in front of his eyes. He stepped back and glanced around, ready to bolt for the door at any second. His eyes focused in on something in the corner that seemed to be moving. He could see it wasn't a person, but an animal. He slowly approached and could see a mama cat and four very small kittens. The mama cat seemed protective and glared at Casey until he put his hand out and just waited for her to come to him. Casey could see the kittens were skinny and needed food. What a surprise it would be to his friends to come out the door with kittens instead of running and screaming!

Name: _____   Date: _____

José's First Day

> **Directions:** Using the Marking Chart as a reference, mark the text below to remind yourself when and how to read it aloud with expression. Then practice reading it aloud, paying special attention to your notes.

This was José's first day of school. All the other students had started months ago, because their parents had normal jobs, and those kids had a normal life. But, not José. His dad was in the military, and it seemed lately they were moving every few months. José knew he wouldn't be able to make friends and keep them, so he wasn't even going to try. He knew better. Going to school, doing what they told him, and getting home were his only goals these days. José entered the classroom and sat down, head down on the desk, just waiting for the day to be over. He could see another student stop by his desk, so he glanced up. He was shocked to see Mason, a kid he recognized from fourth grade! Mason's mom was in the military, too, so Mason knew just what he was going through. What a coincidence that here they were, together again in the same class, two states away! José realized that sometimes, even when things seem bad, there might be something good just around the corner!

Name: _____ Date: _____

My Brother

> **Directions:** Using the Marking Chart as a reference, mark the text below to remind yourself when and how to read it aloud with expression. Then practice reading it aloud, paying special attention to your notes.

I love my brother, but sometimes we just don't get along at all. He is always stealing things from me. He calls it borrowing. "Sis, can I borrow two dollars from you? I'm going with my friends to get a hamburger." "No you can't, Steven," I say. "Not until you pay me the ten dollars you already owe me." He just shrugs and looks at me a little funny. Then, as soon as I walk out of my bedroom, he charges in, grabs my money, and shouts to me as he runs outside the house to meet his friends, "Now I owe you twelve!" Did I really say I love my brother?

Name: _____   Date: _____

A Great Day!

Directions: Using the Marking Chart as a reference, mark the text below to remind yourself when and how to read it aloud with expression. Then practice reading it aloud, paying special attention to your notes.

"Ladies and gentlemen, welcome to this afternoon's baseball game between the New York Yankees and the Boston Red Sox."

It was finally happening! My family was actually going to a Major League Baseball game. When we walked into the stadium, it was like walking into another country! The field was the greenest green I have ever seen. There must have been 20,000 fans in the stands. The cheering was so loud we could barely talk with one another. We had to shout! And I never had a hot dog that tasted so good. What a great day! Best of all, my favorite team won! "Dad, when can we go to another game?"

Name: _____   Date: _____

The Dentist

Directions: Using the Marking Chart as a reference, mark the text below to remind yourself when and how to read it aloud with expression. Then practice reading it aloud, paying special attention to your notes.

"Mom," I cried out, "do I really have to go to the dentist today?

Why not tomorrow?" Last week I had my regular checkup, and my

dentist, Dr. Korb, said I had a cavity that needed filling. I hate going

to the dentist. Dr. Korb is really nice, but it is just so hard to sit there

with your mouth open for 30 minutes or more. And then, once your

mouth is open, she sticks all the instruments in to clean, scrape,

drill, and fill. Mom replied, "Shawn, you know you have to get that

tooth of yours fixed as soon as possible. You don't want it to get

worse, do you? We're leaving in 15 minutes, young man. You better

be ready." And so, I prepared to meet my doom!

Name: _____   Date: _____

My Best Friend

> **Directions:** Using the Marking Chart as a reference, mark the text below to remind yourself when and how to read it aloud with expression. Then practice reading it aloud, paying special attention to your notes.

I couldn't believe it when Thomas told me he was moving with his family to California. Thomas was my best friend! We had known each other since kindergarten, and now he was moving away. Why would his family do this? The next day, as we walked to school, Thomas told me more about his family's move. He said that his father had gotten a new job in California that paid more than he made here. Thomas promised that he would write to me regularly. He said that I might even be able to visit him once his family is settled in their new home. Thomas will be moving soon. What am I going to do?

**Fluency Skills
Practiced**

E

Expression

 ✓

A

Automatic
Word Recognition

 ✓

R

Rhythm
and Phrasing

☐

S

Smoothness

 ✓

2.G Letter Writing With Voice

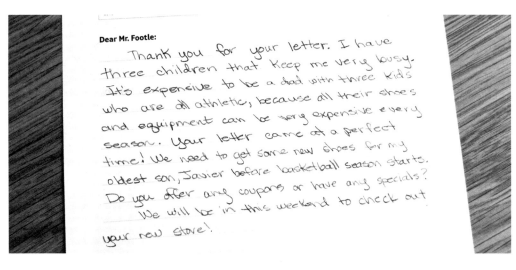

Dear Mr. Footle:

Thank you for your letter. I have three children that keep me very busy. It's expensive to be a dad with three kids who are all athletic, because all their shoes and equipment can be very expensive every season. Your letter came at a perfect time! We need to get some new shoes for my oldest son, Javier before basketball season starts. Do you offer any coupons or have any specials?

We will be in this weekend to check out your new store!

Students read aloud business letters and friendly letters, first for content and then to perform them with appropriate expression, based on the purpose and tone of the letters. From there, they write letters in response and read them orally.

Materials Needed	Copy of a Letter Writing With Voice page for each student, or an overhead projection of a page (pp. 83–91) Pencil for each student
Grades	2–8
Length of Activity	20 minutes
Location	school
Extension Ideas	• Have students do a close reading of the text first to be sure they really understand the meaning. • Invite students to write their own letter and then perform it, focusing on expression.

Business Letter: Arrow Shoe Company

Directions: The following letter was written to convince you to purchase a pair of athletic shoes. Read the letter once to yourself. Does it convince you to buy the shoes? Then practice reading the letter orally in a way the writer of the letter might read it.

Dear Mr./Ms. Hastings:

Are you an athlete? Do you play football with friends? Are you on your school basketball team? Would you like to learn to play tennis? All of these sports require that you be fast on your feet. You'll need to run fast, stop on a dime, and make quick turns. In order to do these things, you need the right athletic shoes.

Fortunately for you, the Arrow Shoe Company is opening a new store on Main and Market Streets. I'd like to personally invite you to come to our store any day after school to take a look at the great selection of shoes we have in stock. We have every color you can imagine. And, best of all, we sell our shoes at a price that you and your family can afford. So, the next time you are on Main Street, stop by the Arrow Shoe Company store and let us sell you the shoes that will help you become the best athlete you can be.

Sincerely,

Anthony Footle

Store Manager

Name: _____ Date: _____

Response to Arrow Shoe Company

Directions: After reading the letter from the point of view of Mr. Footle, write a letter in response. Then practice and perform the letter in a voice that represents the meaning you wish to convey.

Dear Mr. Footle:

_____

_____

_____

_____

_____

_____

_____

_____

_____

_____

_____

_____

_____

Business Letter: Central Cereal Company

Directions: The following letter was written to convince you to work for the Central Cereal Company. Read the letter once to yourself. Does it convince you to go to work for the company? Then practice reading the letter orally in a way the writer of the letter might read it.

Dear Ms./Mr. Semolina:

It is always nice to have some extra spending money. Are you interested in adding to your income? We are a new company in town looking for young people who are interested in adding to their income through a few hours of work every week. Our company, the Central Cereal Company, has developed a new breakfast cereal, called Energy Wheats, that is guaranteed to add energy to any person who has it for breakfast each morning. No more getting up at the crack of dawn feeling tired and drowsy. Now young people who have Energy Wheats will be ready for each new day of school. All we ask is that you put flyers advertising Energy Wheats at the door of all the people who live in your neighborhood. The flyer contains a coupon worth $1.00 off each box of Energy Wheats. Your neighbors will love Energy Wheats, and they will love you for introducing them to this great product. Please call 800-ENR-WHTS if you are interested in working for us. We hope to hear from you very soon.

Sincerely,

Alexa B. Reckfast

Marketing Director

Name: _____   Date: _____

Response to Central Cereal Company

Directions: After reading the letter from the point of view of Alexa B. Reckfast, write a letter in response. Then practice and perform the letter in a voice that represents the meaning you wish to convey.

Dear Ms. Reckfast:

_____

_____

_____

_____

_____

_____

_____

_____

_____

_____

_____

_____

_____

_____

_____

_____

Friendly Letter: Get Well, Jasmine

Directions: The following get-well letter was written by a student. Read it to yourself once. Then practice reading the letter orally in a way that Logan, the writer, might read it.

Dear Jasmine:

I want to send you this note to tell you how much I missed you in school this week. Our teacher says that you have been ill and were told to stay home by your doctor. I sure hope you get well soon; we need you here in school with us! Last week was a pretty tough week in school. We had tests every day, and you know how much I love tests! On the fun side, we had our annual school basketball game between the students and the teachers. Can you believe the students won? I wonder if the teachers let us win. You know Mrs. Smithers is such a good player, and yet she did not make one basket. Well, that's about all that happened last week. Please give me a call at home if you feel like it. I can't wait to see your smiling face again when you're back in school. Take care.

Your friend,

Logan

Name: _____   Date: _____

Response From Jasmine

Directions: After reading the letter in the voice of Logan, write a letter in response from Jasmine. What would Jasmine say to Logan? Then practice and perform the letter in a voice that represents the meaning you want Logan to convey.

Dear Logan:

_____

_____

_____

_____

_____

_____

_____

_____

_____

_____

_____

_____

_____

_____

Friendly Letter: Thank You, Grandma and Grandpa

Directions: The following thank-you letter was written by a young person to her grandparents. Read the letter once to yourself. Then practice reading the letter orally in a way Kim, the writer, might read it.

Dear Grandma and Grandpa:

You are the BEST grandparents ever! I received your birthday card in the mail yesterday. Mom let me open it then, even though my birthday wasn't until today. How did you know that I wanted tickets to the Cranky Keys concert? They are so popular that I didn't think I would even be able to see them. All their concerts in other cities sold out! And yet, you came through for me. Thank you, thank you, thank you! I wish you could go to the concert with me. In fact, I wish you lived closer so that we could see each other more in person rather than having to write letters to each other. Please know how much I love you. I can't wait to see you next month when we come for a visit. I'll tell you all about the concert then.

Love,

Kim

Name: _____ Date: _____

Response From Grandma and Grandpa

Directions: After reading the letter in the voice of Kim, write a letter in response from her grandparents. What would her grandparents say to Kim? Then practice and perform the letter in a voice that represents the meaning you want the grandparents to convey.

Dear Kim:

_____

_____

_____

_____

_____

_____

_____

_____

_____

_____

_____

_____

_____

_____

_____

Name: _____   Date: _____

Write Your Own!

Directions: Write a letter to a friend, family member, or business in which you use your voice to make your point. Once you have written the letter, practice reading it several times until you are able to read it with appropriate expression that expands on the meaning you wish to convey. Perform your letter for one or more members of your class.

**Fluency Skills
Practiced**

E

Expression

A

Automatic
Word Recognition

R

Rhythm
and Phrasing

S

Smoothness

2.H Class Name Poem

Each student writes one line of a poem, following the same structure—for example:

- adjective, your first name, "likes to," verb, adjective, noun

- all words, except "likes to," should start with the same letter.

Example: "Wiggly Wendy likes to wear white watches."

Then combine the lines into a class name poem and have students read it aloud. Consider having students read it daily, for a couple of weeks, until they know it well.

Class Name Poem:
Super Spencer likes to slurp spectacular sauce.
Troubled Taylor likes to talk to turtles.
Daring Deb likes to draw dancing daisies.
Magical MaKayla likes to make music.
Baseball Brandon likes to bake banana bread.
Awesome Addy likes to add ants in Africa.
Popular Peter likes to party with pizza.
Talented Tina likes to tinker with toys
Chocolate Charles likes to chew cheese

Materials Needed	Writing paper for each student Pencil for each student
Grades	2–8
Length of Activity	20 minutes
Location	school
Extension Idea	• Invite students to perform the finished poem for parents at an open house or family night.

2.1 Phrase Lists and Graph

 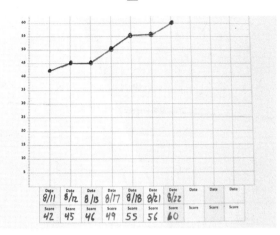

**Fluency Skills
Practiced**

E

Expression

A

Automatic
Word Recognition

R

Rhythm
and Phrasing

S

Smoothness

Using the phrase lists on pages 94 to 99, which were created using high-frequency words, students read in phrases, or in chunks, rather than word-by-word, one list at a time. They then partner up with a classmate at approximately the same reading level. As they read aloud the phrases on a list, you can time them as their partner listens for errors. (We recommend three minutes for younger students and two for older or more fluent readers.) Students can use the graph on page 100 to record their scores in the form of a line graph (words or phrases read correctly in the time period). Do this activity once a day until students can read the entire list within the time period.

Materials Needed	Copy of a Phrase List for each student, in a folder (pp. 94–99) Pencil for each student
Grades	2–6 (or struggling readers in higher grades)
Length of Activity	10–15 minutes each day
Location	school or home
Extension Ideas	• Do this activity as a whole class with younger students and in small groups with older students who may be struggling and need the extra practice. • Train parents on this activity so they can help their child at home. Explaining the activity during a parent conference and sending home the required materials allows parents to be part of their child's success. • While the text may not be that engaging, don't be surprised if students are motivated nonetheless by their progress and success; celebrate improvements with students, whether they're struggling or exceeding expectations. • Depending on grade level, put 10 to 20 phrases on a chart and practice reading them chorally during the week.

List 1

1.	the little boy	26.	he is it	51.	to go home	76.	who am I
2.	a good boy	27.	I can go	52.	see the dog	77.	an old cat
3.	is about me	28.	they are here	53.	then they went	78.	in their car
4.	then you give	29.	one by one	54.	look at us	79.	she has some
5.	was to come	30.	good and wet	55.	yes and no	80.	a new school
6.	old and new	31.	came with me	56.	play with him	81.	he said it
7.	what we know	32.	about a dog	57.	by the house	82.	did not go
8.	that old man	33.	had a hat	58.	he was going	83.	a good boy
9.	in and out	34.	three little dogs	59.	come to me	84.	three little dogs
10.	get the cat	35.	some good cake	60.	get the cat	85.	up and down
11.	good for you	36.	up and down	61.	in or out	86.	go to work
12.	down at work	37.	her green hat	62.	one, two, three	87.	put it out
13.	with his cat	38.	say and do	63.	to the man	88.	we were there
14.	it was over	39.	when they come	64.	a little dog	89.	before you go
15.	work on it	40.	so I went	65.	he has it	90.	just one day
16.	can come here	41.	my little house	66.	sit by them	91.	about this long
17.	they will go	42.	very good girl	67.	how do you	92.	here it is
18.	are so long	43.	all around	68.	like the book	93.	get the other
19.	three of them	44.	would you like	69.	in our car	94.	our old car
20.	before this one	45.	any good book	70.	what do you	95.	then take it
21.	your little boy	46.	have you been	71.	do you know	96.	can use it
22.	as long as	47.	we are out	72.	make a book	97.	again and again
23.	but not me	48.	here and there	73.	which one is	98.	would give him
24.	be here again	49.	from my mother	74.	this much is	99.	day after day
25.	have been good	50.	a nice day	75.	about his frog	100.	many of them

List 2

1.	saw a cat	26.	such a big box	51.	may come to	76.	dog ran fast
2.	he let us	27.	where it was	52.	he let us	77.	five blue balls
3.	write the word	28.	I am not	53.	write the word	78.	read very well
4.	stand on the	29.	a great ball	54.	these big chairs	79.	over the hill
5.	in a box	30.	yesterday morning	55.	turn right at	80.	such a treat
6.	the word is	31.	live in a	56.	the word is	81.	on the way
7.	we should leave	32.	four of them	57.	we should leave	82.	eat too much
8.	came up to	33.	then at last	58.	her left hand	83.	shall sing for
9.	a tall girl	34.	color the box	59.	more people can	84.	my own bed
10.	will not make	35.	putting it away	60.	why not make	85.	most of all
11	find a rock	36.	tall red hat	61.	is done better	86.	sure am happy
12.	because it was	37.	friend of the	62.	it was under	87.	saw a thing
13.	made me mad	38.	to look pretty	63.	while the rain	88.	only for fun
14.	could I go	39.	much to eat	64.	should we do	89.	near the dog
15.	never would come	40.	want to say	65.	never would come	90.	older than him
16.	look at that	41.	one year old	66.	two books each	91.	in the open
17.	is my mother	42.	the white pine	67.	was the best	92.	kind and good
18.	run out of	43.	got a cup	68.	at another time	93.	must go not
19.	at school today	44.	wanted to play	69.	it would seem	94.	high in the
20.	with the people	45.	found his dog	70.	the pretty tree	95.	far and near
21.	all last night	46.	that was left	71.	was her name	96.	both of you
22.	into my room	47.	bring her home	72.	part of it	97.	end of the
23.	begin to say	48.	men were there	73.	the tall oak	98.	would go also
24.	I think that	49.	as you wish	74.	next to the	99.	until we see
25.	on the back	50.	red and black	75.	please come to	100.	call me now

List 3

1.	go ask her	26.	the black hat	51.	off his ship	76.	start the fire
2.	a small tree	27.	in his ear	52.	his sister went	77.	ten little boys
3.	a yellow box	28.	write a letter	53.	my happy mother	78.	was an order
4.	you may show	29.	to try it	54.	once I went	79.	part was missing
5.	it goes there	30.	as for myself	55.	he didn't go	80.	the early bird
6.	please clean this	31.	can no longer	56.	set the table	81.	the fat cat
7.	buy a present	32.	those were clean	57.	round and round	82.	a third team
8.	say thank you	33.	hold on tight	58.	dress the baby	83.	was the same
9.	they will sleep	34.	full of water	59.	fail the test	84.	were in love
10.	open the letter	35.	please carry it	60.	wash the clothes	85.	can you hear
11	jump the wall	36.	eight little ducks	61.	car will start	86.	yesterday he came
12.	by myself	37.	would you sing	62.	always ready to go	87.	eyes are blue
13.	go fly high	38.	food was warm	63.	anything to wear	88.	door was open
14.	please don't run	39.	sit on the	64.	around the yard	89.	clothes are dry
15.	a fast race	40.	the black dog	65.	close the door	90.	through he went
16.	a cold day	41.	can you rise	66.	the bedroom wall	91.	at three o'clock
17.	must call today	42.	hot and cold	67.	gave some money	92.	second not last
18.	does come back	43.	grow the seed	68.	turn the corner	93.	water is warm
19.	a pretty face	44.	do not cut	69.	might be late	94.	the little town
20.	little green box	45.	seven people came	70.	hard, long trail	95.	took off his
21.	go to bed	46.	the pretty woman	71.	go to bed	96.	pair of mittens
22.	I like grown	47.	the funny monkey	72.	fine black line	97.	now getting dark
23.	your red coat	48.	yes it is	73.	along the way	98.	want to keep
24.	six people ran	49.	as he ate	74.	sat on the chair	99.	head and neck
25.	gave a gift	50.	stop your car	75.	I hope you	100.	warm the food

List 4

1.	the story told	26.	time after time	51.	said the word	76.	wear your coat
2.	miss the bus	27.	has come yet	52.	was almost lost	77.	Mr. and Mrs.
3.	with his father	28.	true or false	53.	he quickly thought	78.	in the side
4.	the children moved	29.	above the door	54.	sent the letter	79.	the poor boy
5.	reached the land	30.	still, cool water	55.	receive the gift	80.	lost his book
6.	with an interest	31.	meet me at	56.	had to pay	81.	was cold outside
7.	in the government	32.	since we started	57.	better than nothing	82.	the wind howled
8.	within two feet	33.	a number of	58.	what I need	83.	Mrs. Brown said
9.	the pretty garden	34.	please state your	59.	mean to cry	84.	we learn by
10.	to be done	35.	does it matter	60.	spoke too late	85.	held the book
11	the country house	36.	draw the line	61.	only finished half	86.	the front door
12.	different from them	37.	did you remember	62.	afraid to fight	87.	it was guilt
13.	the bad men	38.	the large hen	63.	was strong enough	88.	in the family
14.	across the ocean	39.	a few came	64.	feel the fur	89.	it all began
15.	a fenced yard	40.	hit the ball	65.	during the storm	90.	clean air is
16.	a winter morning	41.	under the cover	66.	already had gone	91.	young and old
17.	a round table	42.	the open window	67.	to one hundred	92.	was long ago
18.	a bedtime story	43.	store the box	68.	for the week	93.	around the world
19.	because I'm through	44.	in the city	69.	walked between them	94.	the airplane flew
20.	sometimes I run	45.	are we together	70.	hard to change	95.	without his lunch
21.	tried to run	46.	the bright sun	71.	being quickly spent	96.	do not kill
22.	rode the horse	47.	all my life	72.	care and feeding	97.	ready set go
23.	something for her	48.	across the street	73.	the right answer	98.	please stay away
24.	brought the salad	49.	at the party	74.	an interesting course	99.	won't you come
25.	the dancing shoes	50.	suit was ready	75.	voted against it	100.	the paper flower

List 5

1.	hour by hour	**26.**	grade your paper	**51.**	fry an egg	**76.**	spell the word
2.	be glad that	**27.**	my big brother	**52.**	on the ground	**77.**	a beautiful picture
3.	follow my directions	**28.**	remain there until	**53.**	a sunny afternoon	**78.**	the sick cat
4.	you have company	**29.**	glass of milk	**54.**	feed the sheep	**79.**	because a teacher
5.	would you believe	**30.**	several years ago	**55.**	the boat trip	**80.**	will you cry
6.	begin at once	**31.**	the long war	**56.**	plan his work	**81.**	finish the work
7.	do you mind	**32.**	are you able	**57.**	the question is	**82.**	toss and catch
8.	pass the meat	**33.**	please change it	**58.**	the biggest fish	**83.**	the shiny floor
9.	try to reach	**34.**	either you come	**59.**	return the gum	**84.**	a broken stick
10.	next month we	**35.**	change was less	**60.**	call him sir	**85.**	great amounts of
11	at this point	**36.**	train the dog	**61.**	would not tell	**86.**	guess the answer
12.	rest and relax	**37.**	does it cost	**62.**	the huge hill	**87.**	pain the bridge
13.	he sent it	**38.**	in the evening	**63.**	the wet wood	**88.**	in the church
14.	please talk louder	**39.**	sing the note	**64.**	when you add	**89.**	a tall lady
15.	when we want	**40.**	time is past	**65.**	the dripping ice	**90.**	a treat tomorrow
16.	to the bank	**41.**	find her room	**66.**	broke the car	**91.**	ice and snow
17.	ship the box	**42.**	flew overhead	**67.**	watch for children	**92.**	for whom the
18.	his business is	**43.**	at his office	**68.**	left all alone	**93.**	women and children
19.	the whole thing	**44.**	the cow stood	**69.**	to bend low	**94.**	among the leaves
20.	a short stop	**45.**	will you visit	**70.**	broke her arm	**95.**	a rocky road
21.	make certain that	**46.**	wait in line	**71.**	dinner was cold	**96.**	the farm animals
22.	was not fair	**47.**	the teacher said	**72.**	hair is grown	**97.**	my famous cousin
23.	give the reason	**48.**	is almost spring	**73.**	service the car	**98.**	bread and butter
24.	it's almost summer	**49.**	picture was gone	**74.**	in class today	**99.**	gave wrong directions
25.	fill your glass	**50.**	the blue bird	**75.**	was quite short	**100.**	the space age

List 6

1.	became a man	26.	could see herself	51.	demand a pencil	76.	was my aunt
2.	a fat body	27.	have an idea	52.	however you want	77.	her system was
3.	take a chance	28.	drop the pin	53.	in this case	78.	he will lie
4.	act right now	29.	the wide river	54.	can you figure	79.	the cause was
5.	it will die	30.	her smile glowed	55.	increase your work	80.	will she marry
6.	in real life	31.	son and daughter	56.	enjoy your study	81.	it is possible
7.	must speak out	32.	the bat flew	57.	rather than walk	82.	I will study
8.	it already ended	33.	is a fact	58.	sound it out	83.	one thousand more
9.	a good doctor	34.	sort the clothes	59.	eleven comes next	84.	in the pen
10.	please step up	35.	king of hearts	60.	music in words	85.	his condition was
11	all by itself	36.	the dark street	61.	a human being	86.	she said perhaps
12.	had nine lives	37.	kept to themselves	62.	in the count	87.	she will produce
13.	the baby turtle	38.	whose coat is	63.	may the force	88.	it was twelve
14.	minute by minute	39.	study the book	64.	a tomato plant	89.	he rode the
15.	a loud ring	40.	a great fear	65.	can you suppose	90.	is my uncle
16.	who wrote it	41.	move your car	66.	by the law	91.	the labor force
17.	make it happen	42.	she stood outside	67.	was her husband	92.	in public court
18.	let's appear happy	43.	as for himself	68.	just that moment	93.	I will consider
19.	a big heart	44.	the strong man	69.	my favorite person	94.	it happened thus
20.	can swim fast	45.	for they knew	70.	a sad result	95.	was the least
21.	a felt hat	46.	every so often	71.	he could continue	96.	she has power
22.	the fourth hour	47.	toward the end	72.	the lowest price	97.	made a mark
23.	I'll say it	48.	filled with wonder	73.	to serve well	98.	will be president
24.	kept a long time	49.	twenty black birds	74.	the national anthem	99.	a nice voice
25.	a deep well	50.	it was important	75.	wife and mother	100.	must ask whether

Graph

Name: _____   Phrase List: _____

	Date	Date	Date	Date	Date	Date	Date	Date	Date	Date
	Score	Score	Score	Score	Score	Score	Score	Score	Score	Score

2.J **Syllable Pyramids**

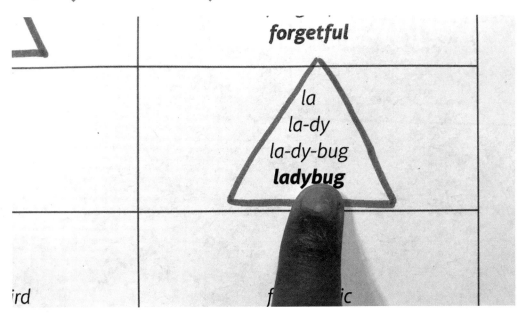

Students read each syllable of a multi-syllable word in a pyramid. Then they reread the syllables and word until they can read the whole pyramid smoothly and fluently. If a child mispronounces a word, quickly and gently correct him or her and continue.

Materials Needed	Copy of a Syllable Pyramids page for each student (pp. 102–108)
Grades	3–8
Length of Activity	10–15 minutes
Location	school or home
Extension Ideas	• Challenge the student to read each word more than three times, or to try to beat his or her time the next day. • Have the student orally create a sentence using each word.

Fluency Skills Practiced

E
Expression

A
Automatic Word Recognition

R
Rhythm and Phrasing

S
Smoothness

Three-Syllable Words

Directions: Read each pyramid top to bottom, adding one syllable at a time to complete the word. Practice reading each pyramid until you can read it smoothly and fluently.

cin cin-na cin-na-mon **cinnamon**	un un-der un-der-stand **understand**
vic vic-to vic-to-ry **victory**	for for-get for-get-ful **forgetful**
de de-cide de-cid-ed **decided**	la la-dy la-dy-bug **ladybug**
hum hum-ming hum-ming-bird **hummingbird**	fan fan-tas fan-tas-tic **fantastic**
um um-brel um-brel-la **umbrella**	li li-brar li-brar-y **library**

Three-Syllable Words

Directions: Read each pyramid top to bottom, adding one syllable at a time to complete the word. Practice reading each pyramid until you can read it smoothly and fluently.

fur fur-ni fur-ni-ture **furniture**	af af-ter af-ter-noon **afternoon**
grand grand-moth grand-moth-er **grandmother**	en en-ve en-ve-lope **envelope**
tel tel-e tel-e-phone **telephone**	de de-vel de-vel-op **develop**
cus cus-to cus-to-mer **customer**	de de-part de-part-ment **department**
lem lem-on lem-on-ade **lemonade**	an an-y an-y-way **anyway**

Four-Syllable Words

Directions: Read each pyramid top to bottom, adding one syllable at a time to complete the word. Practice reading each pyramid until you can read it smoothly and fluently.

cat cat-er cat-er-pil cat-er-pil-lar **caterpillar**	num num-er num-er-a num-er-a-tor **numerator**
re re-spon re-spon-si re-spon-si-ble **responsible**	com com-fort com-fort-a com-fort-a-ble **comfortable**
tel tel-e tel-e-vis tel-e-vis-ion **television**	o o-ver o-ver-whelm o-ver-whelm-ing **overwhelming**
sup sup-er sup-er-he sup-er-he-ro **superhero**	e e-vap e-vap-or e-vap-or-ate **evaporate**
al al-to al-to-geth al-to-geth-er **altogether**	ter ter-min ter-min-a ter-min-a-tion **termination**

Four-Syllable Words

Directions: Read each pyramid top to bottom, adding one syllable at a time to complete the word. Practice reading each pyramid until you can read it smoothly and fluently.

mis mis-un mis-un-der mis-un-der-stand **misunderstand**	dic dic-tion dic-tion-ar dic-tion-ar-y **dictionary**
mac mac-a mac-a-ro mac-a-ro-ni **macaroni**	a a-vo a-vo-cad a-vo-cad-o **avocado**
pop pop-u pop-u-la pop-u-la-tion **population**	cal cal-cu cal-cu-lat cal-cu-lat-or **calculator**
an an-y an-y-bod an-y-bod-y **anybody**	wa wa-ter wa-ter-mel wa-ter-mel-on **watermelon**
al al-li al-li-ga ali-li-ga-tor **alligator**	a a-quar a-quar-i a-quar-i-um **aquarium**

Four-Syllable Words

Directions: Read each pyramid top to bottom, adding one syllable at a time to complete the word. Practice reading each pyramid until you can read it smoothly and fluently.

his his-tor his-tor-i his-tor-i-cal **historical**	mo mo-tor mo-tor-cy mo-tor-cy-cle **motorcycle**
dan dan-de dan-de-li dan-de-li-on **dandelion**	as as-par as-par-a as-par-a-gus **asparagus**
con con-grat con-grat-u con-grat-u-late **congratulate**	cau cau-li cau-li-flow cau-li-flow-er **cauliflower**
in in-vis in-vis-i in-vis-i-ble **invisible**	al al-pha al-pha-be al-pha-be-tize **alphabetize**
hel hel-i hel-i-cop hel-i-cop-ter **helicopter**	A A-mer A-mer-i A-mer-i-ca **America**

Five-Syllable Words

Directions: Read each pyramid top to bottom, adding one syllable at a time to complete the word. Practice reading each pyramid until you can read it smoothly and fluently.

mul mul-ti mul-ti-pli mul-ti-pli-ca mul-ti-pli-ca-tion **multiplication**	qual qual-if qual-if-i qual-if-i-ca qual-if-i-ca-tion **qualification**
un un-i un-i-den un-i-den-ti un-i-den-ti-fied **unidentified**	u u-ni u-ni-ver u-ni-ver-si u-ni-ver-si-ty **university**
in in-tim in-tim-i in-tim-i-dat in-tim-i-dat-ing **intimidating**	com com-mun com-mun-i com-mun-i-ca com-mun-i-ca-tion **communication**
or or-gan or-gan-i or-gan-i-za or-gan-i-za-tion **organization**	fig fig-ur fig-ur-a fig-ur-a-tive fig-ur-a-tive-ly **figuratively**
di di-ag di-ag-on di-ag-on-al di-ag-on-al-ly **diagonally**	per per-son per-son-al per-son-al-i per-son-al-i-ty **personality**

Five-Syllable Words

Directions: Read each pyramid top to bottom, adding one syllable at a time to complete the word. Practice reading each pyramid until you can read it smoothly and fluently.

e e-lec e-lec-tri e-lec-tri-ci e-lec-tri-ci-ty **electricity**	re re-frig re-frig-er re-frig-er-a re-frig-er-a-tor **refrigerator**
an an-ni an-ni-ver an-ni-ver-sa an-ni-ver-sa-ry **anniversary**	im im-ag im-ag-i im-ag-i-na im-ag-i-na-tion **imagination**
pre pre-ci pre-ci-pit pre-ci-pit-a pre-ci-pit-a-tion **precipitation**	in in-di in-di-vid in-di-vid-u in-di-vid-u-al **individual**
bi bi-o bi-o-log bi-o-log-i bi-o-log-i-cal **biological**	cre cre-a cre-a-tiv cre-a-tiv-i cre-a-tiv-i-ty **creativity**
ap ap-prox ap-prox-i ap-prox-i-mate ap-prox-i-mate-ly **approximately**	ap ap-pre ap-pre-ci ap-pre-ci-a ap-pre-ci-a-tion **appreciation**

2.K **Total Tonality**

Fluency Skills Practiced

E
Expression

A
Automatic
Word Recognition

R
Rhythm
and Phrasing

S
Smoothness

Students partner up and take turns reading a phrase, using different voices. The focus is on the tone or nuance of expression, so each reading should sound different.

Materials Needed	Copy of a Total Tonality page for each student (pp. 110–113)
Grades	2–4
Length of Activity	10–15 minutes
Location	school or home
Extension Ideas	• Have students make up their own sentences and come up with ways to read them. Students could also read them, and their partners could guess what emotion they are conveying (scared, happy, etc.). • Use lines from books your students are reading. You can use simple lines, like the ones on the Total Tonality pages, or longer texts.

Creepy Man

Directions: With a partner, take turns reading the phrase in the tone that begins each situation.

Phrase: "Run away from that creepy man!"

	Situation
First read	You are shocked that the man is coming toward you.
Second read	You are angry that the man stole your money.
Third read	You are scared that the man is chasing you and a friend.
Fourth read	You and a friend notice that he's running out of a store with people chasing him.
Fifth read	Come up with your own situation and tone.

Dark Place

Directions: With a partner, take turns reading the phrase in the tone that begins each situation.

Phrase: "It's so dark in this place!"

	Situation
First read	You are underwater. (Put your finger on your lips and wiggle them!)
Second read	You are in a spooky house.
Third read	You are inside the mouth of a whale.
Fourth read	You are a mouse hiding in the wall.
Fifth read	Come up with your own situation and tone.

Eyes Open

Directions: With a partner, take turns reading the phrase in the tone that begins each situation.

Phrase: "I can't keep my eyes open!"

	Situation
First read	You are falling asleep after a long day.
Second read	You are not wanting to look at something scary.
Third read	You are a dinosaur after hunting for food all day.
Fourth read	You are a teenager after working all day.
Fifth read	Come up with your own situation and tone.

Come Inside

Directions: With a partner, take turns reading the phrase in the tone that begins each situation.

Phrase: "Come inside right this minute!"

	Situation
First read	You are a mom or dad yelling to your children because dinner is ready.
Second read	You are a fish telling its owner to put the food in the fish tank.
Third read	You are a teacher yelling at the students because a huge rainstorm is coming.
Fourth read	You are a girl or boy yelling at your friend to come see a dog having puppies.
Fifth read	Come up with your own situation and tone.

Videos and
downloadables
are available at
**Scholastic.com/
FluencyResources.**

Make Fluency Fun: Poems, Songs, Chants, and Other Rhythmic Texts

"Rhythm is sound in motion. It is related to the pulse, the heartbeat, the way we breathe. It rises and falls. It takes us into ourselves; it takes us out of ourselves."

—Edward Hirsch

Have you ever watched a group of children sing a song or perform a poem together? It's likely that, in addition to hearing the children's expressive voices, you also witnessed a sense of community joy as the kids' heads bobbed, feet tapped, and fingers snapped. As human beings, we have this innate sense of rhythm that we find difficult to constrain when reading such texts. We should take advantage of such texts in our reading programs.

Teachers often focus on two major kinds of texts for reading instruction: narrative texts (or stories) and informational texts. While we don't deny that these texts are, indeed, the cornerstones of any reading program, there are other kinds of texts that have been somewhat neglected. Poems, songs, jump-rope chants, tongue twisters, jokes for kids, and other texts add depth and variety to reading. Moreover, the structure of those texts lends itself very well to fluency development. Earlier, we said that fluency is reading with good expression and good phrasing. Rhythmic texts such as poems, songs, and chants are meant to be read with expression and meaningful phrasing. Indeed, linguists often call prosody, the expressive part of oral language, the melody of language. So if we want to nurture prosody, rhythmic texts are a perfect fit.

The unfortunate reality is that with the growing emphasis on informational and narrative texts, rhythmic texts hold a secondary position in the reading curriculum. We regret this. Language, whether oral or written, adds another purpose: to provide joy and entertainment. Think of all the forms of language we encounter on a daily basis that enrich our lives aesthetically. We listen to songs on our digital devices, we attend poetry slams and performances, we hear comedians tell jokes, we see children jumping rope to chants, etc. In all of these instances, there is something about the form of the language that we enjoy. Perhaps it is the melody in the song lyrics, the rhyme in the poetry, the wordplay in the jokes, or the rhythm in the chants. Just as this joyful language is found in everyday life, children should experience it daily in their classrooms as well. In many classrooms we do see songs and poems being performed. However, we're seeing less of it as the emphasis shifts to silent reading of narrative and informational texts.

Some of our best memories from school and home are singing holiday and patriotic songs, reciting silly poems, chanting rhymes on the playground, and delighting in language. We hope you have similar memories, and we want our students to leave school with such memories as well.

Since these texts are meant to be read orally or performed, they are naturals for building reading fluency. They need to be read with appropriate expression, rhythm, and phrasing to be enjoyed and appreciated. In this chapter, we explore ways you can embed joyful language into your classroom and, at the same time, improve your students' reading fluency. If you haven't recently used songs, poems, chants, jokes, cheers, tongue twisters, and the like, we hope that this chapter will inspire you to do so. Make rhythmic texts an integral and joyous part of your reading program!

Strategies

**Fluency Skills
Practiced**

E

Expression

A

Automatic
Word Recognition

R

Rhythm
and Phrasing

S

Smoothness

3.A Silly Songs to Familiar Tunes

Students sing silly songs to familiar tunes that you project for all to see. It helps the first time to go slowly so students can hear all the syllables and pronunciations. Pull out words that may be unfamiliar to students before singing, and discuss their meanings. Repeating the songs daily as a routine, perhaps right after the morning bell or recess, is a great way to focus students before taking on another task. It's also a fun way to integrate repeated readings into the curriculum and strengthen vocabulary.

Materials Needed	Copy of a Silly Songs to Familiar Tunes page (pp. 117–124) projected for students to view and read
Grades	2–8
Length of Activity	10–20 minutes
Location	school or home
Extension Ideas	• Consider these books by Alan Katz, which contain silly songs to familiar tunes: *Are You Quite Polite?*; *Going, Going, Gone! And Other Silly Dilly Sports Songs*; *Take Me Out of the Bathtub and Other Silly Dilly Songs*; *I'm Still Here in the Bathtub: Brand New Silly Dilly Songs*; *Smelly Locker: Silly Dilly School Songs*; *Where Did They Hide My Presents? Silly Dilly Christmas Songs*. • Check out Robert Pottle's *I'm Allergic to School* as well as his website: www.robertpottle.com/poetry-index.php. • Have students write their own silly songs to familiar tunes. Start by asking them to choose a well-known song, then to choose a topic related to going to school, being a kid, or anything else they know about, write wacky lyrics, and perform their songs!

You Are My Teacher

by Robert Pottle

(Sing to the tune of "You Are My Sunshine.")

You are my teacher. My favorite teacher.

You give me homework that takes all night.

And you ask questions that give me headaches.

It is rare that I get one right.

You are my teacher. My favorite teacher.

You give detentions to everyone.

And you make sure when we're in your classroom

nobody ever has fun.

You are my teacher. My favorite teacher.

I'm glad that you have so many rules.

I hope that you'll be my teacher next year.

And oh, by the way, April Fools'.

You Are My Student

by Robert Pottle

(Sing to the tune of "You Are My Sunshine.")

You are my student. My favorite student.

You give me apples that have a worm.

And when I say to be still and quiet

you wiggle and giggle and squirm.

You are my student. My favorite student.

You never listen to what I say.

You don't do homework. You don't behave well.

You're always in trouble all day.

You are my student. My favorite student.

I'm really glad you ignore my rules.

I wish that all kids would act like you do

and oh, by the way, April Fools'.

A Day Off for Sunshine

(Sing to the tune of "Twinkle, Twinkle, Little Star.")

When it's snowy and school is called off

We don't complain, we don't scoff

Sometimes we play in the snow all day

Then sometimes we ride and have fun on our sleigh

But, most of the time we are stuck inside

It's too cold and we're bored and tired.

Tomorrow when I go back to school

I'll suggest we make a new rule

Taking days off only when it snows

Is something now I truly oppose

It would be better, yes most divine

To take a day off just for the sunshine.

Mom, You Aren't Fourteen!

(Sing to the tune of "Do Your Ears Hang Low?")

Do you want to run away

When your mom thinks it's Broadway

And she tries to sing the songs

just to act like she belongs;

half the words she says are wrong

Oh, why is this song so long

Mom, you aren't fourteen!

Do you want to jump off your seat

When she tries to post a tweet

Even though she's having fun,

That won't be the word on the street;

Her behavior is so bad

Hopefully it's just a fad

Mom, you aren't fourteen!

Do you want to make a stink

When your mom dyes her hair pink

This is only getting worse

Now what will my classmates think;

When she drops me off at school,

Instead of being called a fool

They say, "Your mom is cool!"

He's Always on His Phone

(Sing to the tune of "Row, Row, Row Your Boat.")

Click, click, clickity-clack

I hear it then I moan

All day from my brother's room

He's always on his phone.

Ring, ring, ringity-ring

Who is calling now?

Someone else that I don't know

He's always on his phone.

Snap, snap, snappity-snap

He's taking "selfies" alone

He should have enough by now

He's always on his phone.

Buzz, buzz, buzzity-buzz

He's changing his ringtone

Who knew someone could be obsessed

He's always on his phone.

Raising My Hand

(Sing to the tune of "The Alphabet Song.")

Teachers told me I must learn

to raise my hand and wait my turn

Always the same, not one time

Something so boring should be a crime

Maybe there's another way

To be called on when I have something to say.

Shake my head or tap my nose

cross my eyes or wiggle my toes

stomp my feet or clap really loud

other things should be allowed

Any of these are more appealing

How can I change this silly routine?

I'll suggest this, maybe it'll stick

Changing this around should be really quick

I should tell the teacher my plan

Right away before I'm a madman

Excitedly, I raise my hand

And realize I ruined my whole plan!

Yankee Doodle Ditched the Pony

(Sing to the tune of "Yankee Doodle.")

Yankee Doodle went to town,
Riding on a freight train
The click-clack noise was much too loud,
He thought he might go insane.

Yankee Doodle went to town,
Riding on a subway
He missed his stop, had to come back,
He couldn't find the right way.

Yankee Doodle went to town,
Riding on a scooter
He fell three times, got all banged up,
He'd rather ride the commuter.

Yankee Doodle went to town,
Riding on a skateboard
He crashed into an officer,
And now he has a record.

Yankee Doodle went to town,
Riding on a surfboard
On land it didn't work so well,
It might as well be cardboard.

Yankee Doodle went to town,
Riding on a big wheel
He left at noon, got nowhere soon,
He'll never get his next meal.

Yankee Doodle went to town,
Riding on a trolley
The bells, the dings were bothersome,
He didn't feel so jolly.

So…Yankee Doodle went to town,
Riding on his pony
He missed his pony after all,
He mounted then called out "Whoopee!"

Bedtimes Stink

(Sing to the tune of "Three Blind Mice.")

Bedtimes stink

Bedtimes stink

I'm wide awake

Give me a break

Eight o'clock comes way too soon

Wasn't it just half past noon?

The sun left and now it's just the moon

My bedtime stinks.

Bedtimes stink

Bedtimes stink

My eyes won't shut

I think I'm in a rut

I've already tried counting sheep

I've seen them jump, skip, curtsey, and leap

Why won't the sheep just try and fall asleep?

My bedtime stinks.

Bedtimes stink

Bedtimes stink

Why must I yawn?

It's almost dawn (or the night is almost gone?)

My eyes feel droopy, they start to close

Everything settles, my body slows

I think I might actually want to doze

My bedtime......zzzzzz.

3.B **Poems for Many Voices**

Students work in small groups or the whole group broken into parts. Students identify how lines are broken up, based on the directions on the page. Note that texts are read top to bottom or as indicated.

Materials Needed	Copy of a Poems for Many Voices page for each student (pp. 126–130)
Grades	2–8
Length of Activity	5–10 minutes
Location	school
Extension Ideas	• Have students write their own original poems, or take poems already written and change them into poems for two voices • Consider using books with poems for two or more voices: *Big Talk: Poems for Four Voices* by Paul Fleischman *I Am Phoenix: Poems for Two Voices* by Paul Fleischman *Joyful Noise: Poems for Two Voices* by Paul Fleischman *Messing Around on the Monkey Bars: and Other School Poems for Two Voices* by Betsy Franco *Partner Poems for Building Fluency: Grades 4–6* by Timothy V. Rasinski, David L. Harrison, and Gay Fawcett *Partner Poems for Building Fluency, Grades 2-4*, by Bobbi Katz *Seeds, Bees, Butterflies and More!* by Carole Gerber *You Read to Me, I'll Read to You: Very Short Fables to Read Together* by Mary Ann Hoberman *You Read to Me, I'll Read to You: Very Short Fairy Tales to Read Together* by Mary Ann Hoberman *You Read to Me, I'll Read to You: Very Short Stories to Read Together* by Mary Ann Hoberman

Fluency Skills Practiced

E
Expression

A
Automatic
Word Recognition

R
Rhythm
and Phrasing

S
Smoothness

Directions: Get into four groups and recite your part when it's your turn. Practice repeatedly to improve smoothness.

I Went Fishing

Voice 1	Voice 2	Voice 3	Voice 4
I went fishing.			
	Took some bait.		
		Didn't go early,	
			Didn't go late.
Caught eight fishes			
	To put in my pail.		
		Seven were mackerel,	
			But the eighth was a whale.
The seven were easy			
	To put into the tin,		
		But that whale caused me trouble	
			Before I packed him in!
Took my catch home.			
	What did Mother say?		
		"Get those eight fish out of here—	
			We're having steak today!"

Directions: Get into three groups and recite your part when it's your turn. Boldfaced lines are read with all voices. Practice repeatedly to improve smoothness.

On Top of Spaghetti

Voice 1	Voice 2	Voice 3
On top of spaghetti,	All covered with cheese,	
		I lost my poor meatball
When somebody sneezed.		
It rolled off the table	And onto the floor,	
		And then my poor meatball
Rolled right out the door!		
It rolled in a garden	And under a bush.	
		Now my poor meatball
Was nothing but mush.		
The mush was as tasty	As tasty could be.	
		Early next summer
It grew into a tree.		
The tree was all covered	With beautiful moss.	
		It grew lovely meatballs
In a tomato sauce.		
So if you like spaghetti	All covered with cheese,	
		Hold on to your meatballs
And DON'T EVER SNEEZE!.... AAAAAACHOOOOOOO!		

Directions: Get into three groups and recite your part when it's your turn. Boldfaced lines are read with all voices. Practice repeatedly to improve smoothness.

The Ants Go Marching

Voice 1	Voice 2	Voice 3
The ants go marching one by one, The ants go marching one by one, The ants go marching one by one,	Hurrah, hurrah. Hurrah, hurrah.	 The little one stops to suck his thumb.
And they all go marching down to the ground, to get out of the rain.		
The ants go marching two by two, The ants go marching two by two, The ants go marching two by two,	Hurrah, hurrah. Hurrah, hurrah.	 The little one stops to tie his shoe.
And they all go marching down to the ground, to get out of the rain.		
The ants go marching three by three, The ants go marching three by three, The ants go marching three by three,	Hurrah, hurrah. Hurrah, hurrah.	 The little one stops to climb a tree.
And they all go marching down to the ground, to get out of the rain.		
The ants go marching four by four, The ants go marching four by four, The ants go marching four by four,	Hurrah, hurrah. Hurrah, hurrah.	 The little one stops to shut the door.
And they all go marching down to the ground, to get out of the rain.		

The ants go marching five by five	Hurrah, hurrah.	
The ants go marching five by five	Hurrah, hurrah.	
The ants go marching five by five		The little one stops to take a dive.

And they all go marching down to the ground, to get out of the rain.

The ants go marching six by six,	Hurrah, hurrah.	
The ants go marching six by six,	Hurrah, hurrah.	
The ants go marching six by six,		The little one stops to pick up sticks.

And they all go marching down to the ground, to get out of the rain.

The ants go marching seven by seven,	Hurrah, hurrah.	
The ants go marching seven by seven,	Hurrah, hurrah.	
The ants go marching seven by seven,		The little one stops to pray to heaven.

And they all go marching down to the ground, to get out of the rain.

The ants go marching eight by eight,	Hurrah, hurrah.	
The ants go marching eight by eight,	Hurrah, hurrah.	
The ants go marching eight by eight,		The little one stops to roller skate.

And they all go marching down to the ground, to get out of the rain.

The ants go marching nine by nine,	Hurrah, hurrah.	
The ants go marching nine by nine,	Hurrah, hurrah.	
The ants go marching nine by nine,		The little one stops to check the time.

And they all go marching down to the ground, to get out of the rain.

The ants go marching ten by ten,	Hurrah, hurrah.	
The ants go marching ten by ten,	Hurrah, hurrah.	
The ants go marching ten by ten,		The little one stops to shout, "The End."

And they all go marching down to the ground, to get out of the rain.

Directions: Get into four groups and recite your part when it's your turn. Practice repeatedly to improve smoothness.

The Gettysburg Address

(excerpt)
by Abraham Lincoln, adapted by Melissa Cheesman Smith

Voice 1	Voice 2	Voice 3	Voice 4
we cannot dedicate			
	dedicate		
		we cannot consecrate	
			consecrate
we cannot hallow this ground The brave men,	hallow this ground	hallow this ground	hallow this ground
	living and dead		
		who struggled here	
			have consecrated it
		far above	
	our poor power		
to add or detract The world			
	will little note		
		nor long remember	
what we say here but	what we say here	what we say here	what we say here
	but		
		but	
			but
it can never forget		it can never forget	
	what they did here.		what they did here.
It is for us			
	the living, rather,		
		to be dedicated here	
			dedicated here
to the unfinished work			
	which they		
		who fought here	
			have thus
far so nobly advanced	far so nobly advanced	far so nobly advanced	far so nobly advanced

3.C **Jump-Rope Chants**

**Fluency Skills
Practiced**

E
Expression

A
Automatic
Word Recognition

R
Rhythm
and Phrasing

S
Smoothness

Students practice reading aloud jump-rope chants with rhythm and expression. Each chant should be practiced multiple times to improve smoothness.

Materials Needed	Copy of Jump-Rope Chants page for each student, or projected (pp. 132–136)
Grades	2–8
Length of Activity	10–15 minutes
Location	school or home
Extension Ideas	• Have students do the chants while jump roping once they know them well. • Invite students to find the beat of each chant by clapping their hands or patting their legs or desk while doing the chant. • Check out this book if you're looking for more chants: *Anna Banana: 101 Jump-Rope Rhymes* by Joanna Cole.

Directions: Read aloud the chant with expression, capturing its rhythm.

I Know Something

I know something,

But I won't tell.

Three little monkeys,

in a peanut shell.

One can read,

And one can dance,

And one has a hole,

in the seat of his pants!

Directions: Read aloud the chant with expression, capturing its rhythm.

Teddy Bear

Teddy Bear, Teddy Bear,
Turn around.

Teddy Bear, Teddy Bear,
Touch the ground.

Teddy Bear, Teddy Bear,
Touch your shoe.

Teddy Bear, Teddy Bear,
That will do.

Teddy Bear, Teddy Bear,
Turn out the light.

Teddy Bear, Teddy Bear,
Say good night!

Apples and Pears

Johnny gave me apples,

Johnny gave me pears.

Johnny gave me fifty cents

To kiss him on the stairs.

I gave him back his apples,

I gave him back his pears.

I gave him back his fifty cents

And kicked him down the stairs.

Directions: Read aloud the chant with expression, capturing its rhythm.

I Had a Little Puppy

I had a little puppy.

His name was Tiny Tim.

I put him in the bathtub,

To see if he could swim.

He drank up all the water.

He ate a bar of soap.

The next thing you know,

He had a bubble in his throat.

In came the doctor

In came the nurse

In came the lady

With the alligator purse.

Out went the doctor

Out went the nurse

Out went the lady

With the alligator purse.

Directions: Read aloud the chant with expression, capturing its rhythm.

Miss Mary Mack

Miss Mary Mack, Mack, Mack

All dressed in black, black, black

With silver buttons, buttons, buttons

All down her back, back, back.

She asked her mother, mother, mother,

For fifteen cents, cents, cents,

To see the elephant, elephant, elephant,

Jump over the fence, fence, fence.

He jumped so high, high, high.

He reached the sky, sky, sky,

And he never came back, back, back

Till the Fourth of July, lie, lie.

3.D **Tongue Twisters**

Copy and cut out the tongue twisters that appear on pages 138 to 141 and give one to each student. Students practice their tongue twisters on their own and then perform them in small groups or in front of the class.

Fluency Skills Practiced

E

Expression

☐

A

Automatic Word Recognition

☐

R

Rhythm and Phrasing

☑

S

Smoothness

☑

Materials Needed	Copy of one Tongue Twister for each student (pp. 138–141)
Grades	2–8
Length of Activity	10–15 minutes
Location	school or home
Extension Ideas	• Have students practice saying the tongue twisters in different ways: really fast three times in a row, with an accent, etc. • Invite students to walk around while music is playing and quickly trade cards with someone else. Students continue to trade until the music stops, and then they practice reading the card in their hand. Repeat several times so students try multiple tongue twisters. • Find even more tongue twisters in Jon Agee's wonderful book, *Orangutan Tongs: Poems to Tangle Your Tongue.*

Tongue Twisters

Tongue Twister 1:

Willie's really weary.

Tongue Twister 2:

Twitching, walking witches talking.

Tongue Twister 3:

Shriek, screak, squawk, and squeak.

Tongue Twister 4:

Rubber baby buggy bumper.

Tongue Twister 5:

Big bad bugs bit Bitsy's back.

Tongue Twister 6:

Sixty silly sisters simply singing.

Tongue Twister 7:

Quick throats, thick quotes.

Tongue Twister 8:

A quick-witted cricket critic.

Tongue Twister 9:

Tie twine to three tree twigs.

Tongue Twister 10:

Willy's real rear wheel.

Tongue Twister 11:

Frogfeet, flippers, swimfins.

Tongue Twister 12:

Skateboarders scream, skeletons scream, the school screams for ice cream!

Tongue Twister 13:

Seventy-seven benevolent elephants.

Tongue Twister 14:

How can a clam cram in a clean cream can?

Tongue Twister 15:

Black background, brown background.

Tongue Twister 16:

Gobbling gargoyles gobbled gobbling goblins.

Tongue Twister 17:

Six sleek swans swam swiftly southwards.

Tongue Twister 18:

The instinct of an extinct insect stinks.

Tongue Twister 19:

Six sick hicks nick six slick bricks with picks and sticks.

Tongue Twister 20:

Fred fed Ted bread, and Ted fed Fred bread.

Tongue Twister 21:

Thin sticks, thick bricks.

Tongue Twister 22:

Wayne went to Wales to watch walruses.

Tongue Twister 23:

He threw three free throws.

Tongue Twister 24:

A big black bear sat on a big black rug.

Tongue Twister 25:

Can you can a can as a canner can can a can?

Tongue Twister 26:

Five fine Florida florists fried fresh flat flounder fish fillet.

Tongue Twister 27:

I slit the sheet, the sheet I slit, and on the slitted sheet I sit.

Tongue Twister 28:

We surely shall see the sun shine soon.

Tongue Twister 29:

Imagine managing the manger at an imaginary menagerie.

Tongue Twister 30:

If Stu chews shoes, should Stu choose the shoes he chews?

Tongue Twister 31:

A cuckoo cookie cook called Cooper could cook cuckoo cookies.

Tongue Twister 32:

Lesser leather never weathered wetter weather better.

Tongue Twister 33:

Which witch wishes to switch a witch wristwatch for a Swiss wristwatch?

Tongue Twister 34:

A three-toed tree toad loved a two-toed he-toad that lived in a too-tall tree.

Tongue Twister 35:

I have got a date at a quarter to eight; I'll see you at the gate, so don't be late.

Tongue Twister 36:

The skunk sat on a stump and thunk the stump stunk, but the stump thunk the skunk stunk.

Tongue Twister 37:

If a noisy noise annoys an onion, an annoying noisy noise annoys an onion more!

Tongue Twister 38:

How much wood would a woodchuck chuck,

If a woodchuck could chuck wood?

He would chuck, he would, as much as he could,

And chuck as much wood as a woodchuck would

If a woodchuck could chuck wood.

Tongue Twister 39:

Peter Piper picked a peck of pickled peppers. Did Peter Piper pick a peck of pickled peppers?

If Peter Piper picked a peck of pickled peppers, where's the peck of pickled peppers Peter Piper picked?

Tongue Twister 40:

When a doctor doctors a doctor, does the doctor doing the doctoring doctor as the doctor being doctored wants to be doctored or does the doctor doing the doctoring doctor as he wants to doctor?

Fluency Skills Practiced

E

Expression

☑

A

Automatic Word Recognition

☑

R

Rhythm and Phrasing

☑

S

Smoothness

☑

3.E **Kid Jokes**

Teach students how to read a joke using the tips and examples as shown in the anchor chart to the left. Copy and cut out the jokes that appear on pages 143 to 146, and lay them facedown on a table. Students choose a joke and practice reading it, focusing on delivering the punch line without hesitations. They continue to walk around the table and "trade jokes," getting better each time they read one aloud. Then have students read aloud their jokes to peers or parents and, if the audience can't guess it, deliver the punch line.

Materials Needed	Copy of one Kid Jokes for each student (pp. 143–146)
Grades	2–8
Length of Activity	10–15 minutes
Location	school or home
Extension Ideas	• Invite students to look up other jokes on the Internet to use. • Give students a homework assignment to either research or write a joke to bring to class the next day. Have students repeat the activity.

Kid Jokes

Kid Joke 1:

When do you go at red and stop at green?

When you're eating a watermelon.

Kid Joke 2:

Why can't your nose be 12 inches long?

Because then your nose would be a foot.

Kid Joke 3:

Why did the math book look so sad?

Because it had so many problems.

Kid Joke 4:

Why couldn't the pirate play cards?

Because he was sitting on the deck.

Kid Joke 5:

What do you call a bear with no teeth?

A gummy bear.

Kid Joke 6:

Why did the robber take a bath before he robbed the bank?

Because he wanted to make a clean getaway.

Kid Joke 7:

Why do you go to bed every night?

Because the bed won't come to you.

Kid Joke 8:

How did the barber win the race?

He knew a short cut.

Kid Joke 9:

What did one wall say to the other wall?

I'll meet you at the corner.

Kid Joke 10:

How do you make a fire with two sticks?

Make sure one of them is a match.

Kid Joke 11:

What stays on the ground but never gets dirty?

A shadow.

Kid Joke 12:

What do you call a pig that knows karate?

A pork chop.

Kid Joke 13:

What is a pretzel's favorite dance?

The Twist.

Kid Joke 14:

What did zero say to eight?

I like your belt.

Kid Joke 15:

What does a nosey pepper do?

It gets jalapeño business.

Kid Joke 16:

What kind of music are balloons scared of?

Pop music.

Kid Joke 17:

What is the ideal date night for cows?

Dinner and a MOO-vie.

Kid Joke 18:

What goes up but never comes down?

Your age.

Kid Joke 19:

Why do golfers bring an extra pair of pants?

In case they get a hole in one.

Kid Joke 20:

Why didn't Cinderella make the basketball team?

She always ran away from the ball.

Kid Joke 21:

What do you give a sick lemon?

Lemon-"aid."

Kid Joke 22:

Why couldn't the pony sing himself to sleep with a lullaby?

Because he was a little hoarse.

Kid Joke 23:

How does the ocean say hello?

It waves.

Kid Joke 24:

What do you call an alligator in a vest?

An investigator.

Kid Joke 25:

What goes up and down but does not move?

Stairs.

Kid Joke 26:

What do you call a story about a broken pencil?

A pointless story.

Kid Joke 27:

What type of button does not unbutton?

A belly button.

Kid Joke 28:

What kind of shoes do frogs wear?

Open-toad shoes.

Kid Joke 29:

What do you call cheese that is not yours?

Nacho cheese.

Kid Joke 30:

Why are ghosts bad liars?

Because you can see right through them.

Kid Joke 31:

What's worse than finding a worm in the apple you are eating?

Finding half a worm.

Kid Joke 32:

What sound do porcupines make when they kiss?

Ouch!

Kid Joke 33:

What object is king of the classroom?

The ruler.

Kid Joke 34:

Why did the football coach go to the bank?

To get his quarterback.

Kid Joke 35:

What did one candle say to the other candle?

I'm going out tonight.

Kid Joke 36:

Why was the boy sitting on his watch?

Because he wanted to be on time.

Kid Joke 37:

What do you get when you cross a snake and a pie?

A "pie"thon (python).

Kid Joke 38:

What kind of table can you eat?

A vegetable.

Kid Joke 39:

Why don't skeletons fight each other?

They don't have the guts.

Kid Joke 40:

Why didn't the sun go to college?

Because it already had a million degrees.

3.F Character Expression

Students read aloud a short paragraph in a voice that captures the mood of the paragraph. Then they will try reading it in other voices.

Materials Needed	Copy of a Character Expression page for each student (pp. 148–151) Pencil for each student
Grades	2–8
Length of Activity	10–15 minutes
Location	school or home
Extension Ideas	• Encourage students to brainstorm other voices in which they could read the paragraphs. • Have students write and then read in an appropriate voice their own response to the original text.

Fluency Skills Practiced

E
Expression

A
Automatic Word Recognition

R
Rhythm and Phrasing

S
Smoothness

A Beautiful Morning

Directions: Read aloud the following paragraph in the voice of a person enjoying a beautiful morning.

I woke up this morning with the sun shining through my bedroom window. Oh, my, I thought to myself, today is going to be a wonderful day. I dressed quickly and walked outside to my backyard. Bees were buzzing, birds were chirping, squirrels were scurrying about! It seemed as if my yard had come to life. The sun was warm, and the gentle breeze felt like nature patting my cheek. I wish all mornings could be like this.

What other voices could you use? Tired and grumpy? Confused?

Bonus: Write a description of a not-so-nice morning. Then read your description in a sad, hopeless voice.

Calling A-1 Video Games

Directions: Read aloud the following paragraph in the voice of a person complaining on the telephone to a video game company that sent her or him the wrong item.

Hello, is this A-1 Video Games? Last week I ordered your *Space Trackers* video game. I was really excited to receive it in the mail yesterday. Unfortunately, you sent me the wrong game. Can you believe it? Instead of *Space Trackers*, you sent me *Space Trekkers*! I already have *Space Trekkers*, and I don't want another version of the same game. What do I have to do to get my order corrected?

What other voices could you use to read this paragraph? Upbeat and positive? Very tired?

Bonus: Write the response that the caller receives from A-1 Video Games. Then read the response in the voice of a representative from the company.

12-Hour Energy Bar Commercial

Directions: Read aloud the following paragraph in the voice of a person who is advertising energy bars on television or radio.

Do you feel tired most of the time? Do you feel like you do not have enough energy to do all the things that you need to do? Why not try our new product called 12-Hour Energy Bars? Eat just one of these delicious bars, and you will find yourself with more than enough energy to make it through the day. Our bars contain a secret ingredient that was only recently discovered in the Amazon jungles. We guarantee that one 12-Hour Energy Bar each day will take away those tired feelings and give you the strength and energy that you need.

What other voices could you use to read this paragraph? Disappointed that the bars didn't work? Totally wired because the bars worked too well?

Bonus: After having tried 12-Hour Energy Bars, write a note to the company about what you think of the product. Then read your note in a voice that reflects how you feel.

Child Pleads With Mom to Go to a Movie

Directions: Read aloud the following paragraph in the voice of a child who is pleading with his mother to allow him to go to a movie with a friend.

Mom, please, please, please. Please, can I go with Kim to the movie theater tonight? I promise I will get all my homework done before we go. I will get all my chores done too—promise! I will even pay my own way to get in the theater. I just have to see *Return From Mars*! If I don't, I'll be the only person in my class who has not seen it. Please, Mommy, please.

What other character voices could you use to read this paragraph? The brother or sister of the child who is asking the mother to go to the movie? The brother or sister who is mocking how the child pleaded with the mother, to a friend?

Bonus: Write the mother's response to the child's request. Then read the response in the voice of the mother.

CHAPTER 4

Make Fluency
Social: Choral
Reading and
Echo-Reading

Videos and
downloadables
are available at
Scholastic.com/
FluencyResources.

CHAPTER 4

Make Fluency Social: Choral Reading and Echo-Reading

"Choral reading is a wonderful way to build community in the classroom."

—Timothy V. Rasinski

We often think of reading as a solitary act. We read primarily for our own purposes. However, reading is also a social act. When we read we are communicating, in a sense, with the author. When we chat with others about what we have read, again, we make reading social.

Our work in schools is not only to develop students skilled in academic content, but also to help them become social beings and good citizens. Working cooperatively with others is a great way to achieve that.

The act of reading with oral expression is a social, or community, activity. Every morning in classrooms around the United States, students read and recite in unison the Pledge of Allegiance. In other countries, similar forms of choral reading and recitation occur. Research tells us that one of the best ways to develop fluency is to read with others (particularly those who may be more fluent than ourselves) (Rasinski, 2010; Rasinski, Reutzel, Chard, & Linan-Thompson, 2011). This form of community reading allows the more fluent readers to support the less fluent readers, thus leading them to higher levels of fluency.

Choral reading is perhaps the most common form of community reading. In its most basic form it involves multiple readers reading the same text orally, with the more fluent readers supporting the less fluent. What is great about choral reading is that it can take many forms. In this chapter we provide you with a wide variety of options that will allow you to add variety to your reading program and choose forms of choral reading that are most appropriate for different texts.

When students feel that they are part of a team, rather than in competition with each other, they are more likely to engage in collaborative learning and become better classroom and community citizens. Choral reading is one way to make that collaborative community a reality and, at the same time, improve students' reading.

Strategies

4.A	**Unison Choral Reading** Read in unison as a class.	154
4.B	**Refrain Choral Reading** One student reads while class reads refrain or repeated text.	159
4.C	**Cumulative Choral Reading** Number of students reading increases as the text progresses.	166
4.D	**Solo Line Choral Reading** Class reads while solo reader reads individual line assigned.	171
4.E	**Call-and-Response Choral Reading** Two groups: one group does a "call," the other a "response."	176
4.F	**Simultaneous Choral Reading** Two groups: one group reads the full text, the other repeats a phrase.	181
4.G	**Line-a-Child Choral Reading** Each student is assigned an individual line, but a few lines are read together.	184
4.H	**Impromptu Choral Reading** Students individually choose the line they want to read.	189
4.I	**Echo-Reading** Teacher or student reads a line while class echoes.	194
4.J	**Reverse Echo-Reading** Two groups: one group reads a line, the other echoes it.	199

**Fluency Skills
Practiced**

E

Expression

☐

A

Automatic
Word Recognition

☑

R

Rhythm
and Phrasing

☑

S

Smoothness

☑

4.A **Unison Choral Reading**

Read in unison as a class.

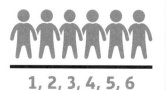

1, 2, 3, 4, 5, 6

> **Twinkle, Twinkle, Little Star**
> 1. Twinkle, twinkle, little star
> 2. How I wonder what you are
> 3. Up above the world so high
> 4. Like a diamond in the sky
> 5. Twinkle, twinkle, little star
> 6. How I wonder what you are

Students read aloud classic texts in unison, as a class. Those who are usually shy or self-conscious about reading aloud will feel supported by having classmates reading right along with them. Feedback is "built-in" as students hear other students around them reading and try to mirror the reading in unison.

Materials Needed	Copy of a Unison Choral Reading page projected in class for all students to view and read (pp. 155–158)
Grades	2–8
Length of Activity	5–10 minutes depending on length of text
Location	school or home
Extension Idea	• Practice the text in class, then send a copy home so students can practice with an older sibling, partner, or guardian. Require students to read it a certain number of times, then have a parent/guardian sign and return it to class to check off that the homework was completed.

Directions: Read aloud this poem as a group, focusing on reading smoothly.

The New Colossus

by Emma Lazarus

Not like the brazen giant of Greek fame,

With conquering limbs astride from land to land;

Here at our sea-washed, sunset gates shall stand

A mighty woman with a torch, whose flame

Is the imprisoned lightning, and her name

Mother of Exiles. From her beacon-hand

Glows world-wide welcome; her mild eyes command

The air-bridged harbor that twin cities frame.

"Keep, ancient lands, your storied pomp!" cries she

With silent lips. "Give me your tired, your poor,

Your huddled masses yearning to breathe free,

The wretched refuse of your teeming shore.

Send these, the homeless, tempest-tost to me,

I lift my lamp beside the golden door!"

> **Directions**: Read aloud this portion of the United States Constitution as a group, focusing on reading smoothly.

The Preamble

We the people of the United States,

in order to form a more perfect union,

establish justice, insure domestic tranquility,

provide for the common defense,

promote the general welfare,

and secure the blessings of liberty to ourselves

and our posterity,

do ordain and establish this Constitution for the

United States of America.

Directions: Read aloud this "Holy Sonnet" as a group, focusing on reading smoothly.

Death, Be Not Proud

by John Donne

Death, be not proud, though some have called thee

Mighty and dreadful, for thou art not so;

For those whom thou think'st thou dost overthrow

Die not, poor Death, nor yet canst thou kill me.

From rest and sleep, which but thy pictures be,

Much pleasure; then from thee much more must flow,

And soonest our best men with thee do go,

Rest of their bones, and soul's delivery.

Thou art slave to fate, chance, kings, and desperate men,

And dost with poison, war, and sickness dwell,

And poppy or charms can make us sleep as well

And better than thy stroke; why swell'st thou then?

One short sleep past, we wake eternally

And death shall be no more; Death, thou shalt die.

> **Directions**: Read aloud this poem as a group, focusing on reading smoothly.

Stopping by Woods on a Snowy Evening

by Robert Frost

Whose woods these are I think I know.

His house is in the village though;

He will not see me stopping here

To watch his woods fill up with snow.

My little horse must think it queer

To stop without a farmhouse near

Between the woods and frozen lake

The darkest evening of the year.

He gives his harness bells a shake

To ask if there is some mistake.

The only other sound's the sweep

Of easy wind and downy flake.

The woods are lovely, dark and deep,

But I have promises to keep,

And miles to go before I sleep,

And miles to go before I sleep.

4.B Refrain Choral Reading

One student reads while class reads refrain or repeated text.

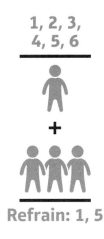

1, 2, 3, 4, 5, 6

+

Refrain: 1, 5

Twinkle, Twinkle, Little Star
1. Twinkle, twinkle, little star
2. How I wonder what you are
3. Up above the world so high
4. Like a diamond in the sky
5. Twinkle, twinkle, little star
6. How I wonder what you are

One student reads or sings the majority of the text, while the whole class joins in at key points, usually a repeated phrase.

Materials Needed	Copy of a Refrain Choral Reading page projected in class for all students to view and read (pp. 160–165)
Grades	2–8
Length of Activity	5–10 minutes depending on length of text
Location	school or home
Extension Ideas	• Practice the text as a class, then send a copy home to practice with an older sibling, partner, or guardian. Require students to read it a certain number of times, then have a parent/guardian sign and return it to class to check off that the homework was completed. • Try "We Shall Not Be Moved" and other texts with repeated phrases.

Fluency Skills Practiced

E
Expression

A
Automatic Word Recognition

R
Rhythm and Phrasing

S
Smoothness

Directions: Read or sing sections of the text labeled "Individual" on your own and have the whole class join in for the boldfaced sections labeled "Refrain—Group."

You Are My Sunshine

Refrain—Group
You are my sunshine, my only sunshine
You make me happy when skies are grey
You'll never know, dear, how much I love you
Please don't take my sunshine away

Individual
The other night, dear, as I lay sleeping
I dreamt I held you in my arms
But when I woke, dear, I was mistaken
And I hung my head, and cried

Refrain—Group
You are my sunshine, my only sunshine
You make me happy when skies are grey
You'll never know, dear, how much I love you
Please don't take my sunshine away

Individual
I'll always love you and make you happy
If you will only say the same
But if you leave me to love another,
You'll regret it all some day

Refrain—Group
You are my sunshine, my only sunshine
You make me happy when skies are grey
You'll never know, dear, how much I love you
Please don't take my sunshine away

Directions: Read or sing the first line of each section on your own and have the whole class join in for the second, boldfaced line.

Hush Little Baby

Hush, little baby, don't say a word,
Papa's gonna buy you a mockingbird.

And if that mockingbird don't sing,
Papa's gonna buy you a diamond ring.

And if that diamond ring turns brass,
Papa's gonna buy you a looking glass.

And if that looking glass gets broke,
Papa's gonna buy you a billy goat.

And if that billy goat don't pull,
Papa's gonna buy you a cart and bull.

And if that cart and bull turn over,
Papa's gonna buy you a dog named Rover.

And if that dog named Rover won't bark.
Papa's gonna buy you a horse and cart.

And if that horse and cart fall down,
**Well, you'll still be the sweetest little
baby in town.**

Directions: Read or sing the second line of each section on your own, and have the whole class join in for the boldfaced lines.

Hickory Dickory Dock

Hickory dickory dock, the mouse ran up the clock.
The clock struck one, the mouse ran down.
Hickory dickory dock.

Hickory dickory dock, the mouse ran up the clock.
The clock struck two, the mouse said "Boo!"
Hickory dickory dock.

Hickory dickory dock, the mouse ran up the clock.
The clock struck three, the mouse said "Whee!!"
Hickory dickory dock.

Hickory dickory dock, the mouse ran up the clock.
The clock struck four, the mouse said, "No more!"
Hickory dickory dock.

Hickory dickory dock, the mouse ran up the clock.
The clock struck five, the mouse arrived.
Hickory dickory dock.

Directions: Read the first line of each section as a whole class and the second line on your own.

One, Two Buckle My Shoe

One, two,

Buckle my shoe;

Three, four,

Knock at the door;

Five, six,

Pick up sticks;

Seven, eight,

Lay them straight;

Nine, ten,

A big fat hen.

> **Directions:** Read the first and last verses, in boldface, as a class. Read on your own the verse from the middle you've been assigned.

The Cremation of Sam McGee

by William Service

There are strange things done in the midnight sun
By the men who moil for gold;
The Arctic trails have their secret tales
That would make your blood run cold;
The Northern Lights have seen queer sights,
But the queerest they ever did see
Was that night on the marge of Lake Lebarge
I cremated Sam McGee.

Student name

Now Sam McGee was from Tennessee, where the cotton blooms and blows.
Why he left his home in the South to roam 'round the Pole, God only knows.
He was always cold, but the land of gold seemed to hold him like a spell;
Though he'd often say in his homely way that "he'd sooner live in hell."

Student name

On a Christmas Day we were mushing our way over the Dawson trail.
Talk of your cold! through the parka's fold it stabbed like a driven nail.
If our eyes we'd close, then the lashes froze till sometimes we couldn't see;
It wasn't much fun, but the only one to whimper was Sam McGee.

Student name

And that very night, as we lay packed tight in our robes beneath the snow,
And the dogs were fed, and the stars o'erhead were dancing heel and toe,
He turned to me, and "Cap," says he, "I'll cash in this trip, I guess;
And if I do, I'm asking that you won't refuse my last request."

Student name

Well, he seemed so low that I couldn't say no; then he says with a sort of moan:
It's the cursèd cold, and it's got right hold till I'm chilled clean through to the bone.
Yet 'tain't being dead—it's my awful dread of the icy grave that pains;
So I want you to swear that, foul or fair, you'll cremate my last remains.

Student name

A pal's last need is a thing to heed, so I swore I would not fail;
And we started on at the streak of dawn; but God! he looked ghastly pale.
He crouched on the sleigh, and he raved all day of his home in Tennessee;
And before nightfall a corpse was all that was left of Sam McGee.

Student name

There wasn't a breath in that land of death, and I hurried, horror-driven,
With a corpse half hid that I couldn't get rid, because of a promise given;
It was lashed to the sleigh, and it seemed to say: "You may tax your brawn and brains,
But you promised true, and it's up to you to cremate those last remains.

Student name

Now a promise made is a debt unpaid, and the trail has its own stern code.
In the days to come, though my lips were dumb, in my heart how I cursed that load.
In the long, long night, by the lone firelight, while the huskies, round in a ring,
Howled out their woes to the homeless snows—O God! how I loathed the thing.

And every day that quiet clay seemed to heavy and heavier grow;
And on I went, though the dogs were spent and the grub was getting low;
The trail was bad, and I felt half mad, but I swore I would not give in;
And I'd often sing to the hateful thing, and it hearkened with a grin.

Till I came to the marge of Lake Lebarge, and a derelict there lay;
It was jammed in the ice, but I saw in a trice it was called the "Alice May."
And I looked at it, and I thought a bit, and I looked at my frozen chum;
Then "Here," said I, with a sudden cry, "is my cre-ma-tor-eum."

Some planks I tore from the cabin floor, and I lit the boiler fire;
Some coal I found that was lying around, and I heaped the fuel higher;
The flames just soared, and the furnace roared—such a blaze you seldom see;
And I burrowed a hole in the glowing coal, and I stuffed in Sam McGee.

Then I made a hike, for I didn't like to hear him sizzle so;
And the heavens scowled, and the huskies howled, and the wind began to blow.
It was icy cold, but the hot sweat rolled down my cheeks, and I don't know why;
And the greasy smoke in an inky cloak went streaking down the sky.

I do not know how long in the snow I wrestled with grisly fear;
But the stars came out and they danced about ere again I ventured near;
I was sick with dread, but I bravely said: "I'll just take a peep inside.
I guess he's cooked, and it's time I looked"; … then the door I opened wide.

And there sat Sam, looking cool and calm, in the heart of the furnace roar;
And he wore a smile you could see a mile, and he said: "Please close that door.
It's fine in here, but I greatly fear you'll let in the cold and storm—
Since I left Plumtree, down in Tennessee, it's the first time I've been warm."

There are strange things done in the midnight sun
By the men who moil for gold;
The Arctic trails have their secret tales
That would make your blood run cold;
The Northern Lights have seen queer sights,
But the queerest they ever did see
Was that night on the marge of Lake Lebarge
I cremated Sam McGee.

Fluency Skills Practiced

E

Expression

[ ]

A

Automatic
Word Recognition

[✓]

R

Rhythm
and Phrasing

[✓]

S

Smoothness

[✓]

4.C **Cumulative Choral Reading**

Number of students reading increases as the text progresses.

Twinkle, Twinkle, Little Star
1. Twinkle, twinkle, little star
2. How I wonder what you are
3. Up above the world so high
4. Like a diamond in the sky
5. Twinkle, twinkle, little star
6. How I wonder what you are

Cumulative choral reading is similar to unison and refrain choral reading, but the class is divided into groups and each group only reads the lines assigned. The number of students reading increases as the text progresses. In other words, one group starts, then another joins in on the next line or passage, then another on the next line or passage, and so forth. With Reverse Cumulative Choral Reading, the opposite happens: the number of students reading decreases as the text progresses. Because cumulative choral reading students must pay attention not only to the whole text, but also to the lines they will read, it requires more focus than regular choral reading.

Materials Needed	Copy of a Cumulative Choral Reading page projected in class for all students to view and read (pp. 167–170)
Grades	2–8
Length of Activity	5–10 minutes depending on the length of text
Location	school or home
Extension Idea	• Practice the text in class, then send a copy home so students can practice with an older sibling, partner, or guardian. Require students to read it a certain number of times, then have a parent/guardian sign and return it to class to check off that the homework was completed.

Directions: Read the passage aloud with your classmates, but only when your part is assigned. Group A starts, and other groups chime in as indicated. Then do the reverse: All groups start, and groups drop off as indicated.

The Gettysburg Address

(beginning)
by Abraham Lincoln

First read:

A	Four score and seven years ago
A, B	our fathers brought forth on this continent
A, B, C	a new nation, conceived in Liberty
A, B, C, D	and dedicated to the proposition that all men are created equal.

Second read:

A, B, C, D	Four score and seven years ago
A, B, C	our fathers brought forth on this continent
A, B	a new nation, conceived in Liberty
A	and dedicated to the proposition that all men are created equal.

Directions: Read the passage aloud with your classmates, but only when your part is assigned. Group A starts, and other groups chime in as indicated. Then do the reverse: All groups start, and groups drop off as indicated.

The Gettysburg Address

(ending)

First read:

A	It is for us the living, rather, to be dedicated here to the unfinished work which they who fought here have thus far so nobly advanced.
A, B	It is rather for us to be here dedicated to the great task remaining before us—that from these honored dead we take increased devotion to that cause for which they gave the last full measure of devotion
A, B, C	that we here highly resolve that these dead shall not have died in vain—that this nation, under God, shall have a new birth of freedom
A, B, C, D	and that government of the people, by the people, for the people, shall not perish from the earth.

Second read:

A, B, C, D	It is for us the living, rather, to be dedicated here to the unfinished work which they who fought here have thus far so nobly advanced.
A, B, C	It is rather for us to be here dedicated to the great task remaining before us—that from these honored dead we take increased devotion to that cause for which they gave the last full measure of devotion
A, B	that we here highly resolve that these dead shall not have died in vain—that this nation, under God, shall have a new birth of freedom
A	and that government of the people, by the people, for the people, shall not perish from the earth.

Directions: Read the passage aloud with your classmates, but only when your part is assigned. Group A starts, and other groups chime in as indicated. Then do the reverse: All groups start, and groups drop off as indicated.

The Pledge of Allegiance

First read:

A	I pledge allegiance to the flag of the United States of America,
A, B	and to the republic for which it stands,
A, B, C	one nation, under God, indivisible,
A, B, C, D	with liberty and justice for all.

Second read:

A, B, C, D	I pledge allegiance to the flag of the United States of America,
A, B, C	and to the republic for which it stands,
A, B	one nation, under God, indivisible,
A	with liberty and justice for all.

Directions: Read the passage aloud with your classmates, but only when your part is assigned. Group 1 starts, and other groups chime in as indicated. Boldfaced words are read by everyone.

The House That Jack Built

	This is the house that Jack built.
1	This is the malt **That lay in the house that Jack built.**
2 1,2	This is the rat, That ate the malt **That lay in the house that Jack built.**
3 2,3 1,2,3	This is the cat, That killed the rat, That ate the malt **That lay in the house that Jack built.**
4 3,4 2,3,4 1,2,3,4	This is the dog, That worried the cat, That killed the rat, That ate the malt **That lay in the house that Jack built.**
5 4,5 3,4,5 2,3,4,5 1,2,3,4,5	This is the cow with the crumpled horn, That tossed the dog, That worried the cat, That killed the rat, That ate the malt **That lay in the house that Jack built.**
6 5,6 4,5,6 3,4,5,6 2,3,4,5,6 1,2,3,4,5,6	This is the maiden all forlorn, That milked the cow with the crumpled horn, That tossed the dog, That worried the cat, That killed the rat, That ate the malt **That lay in the house that Jack built.**

7 6,7 5,6,7 4,5,6,7 3,4,5,6,7 2,3,4,5,6,7 1,2,3,4,5,6,7	This is the man all tattered and torn, That kissed the maiden all forlorn, That milked the cow with the crumpled horn, That tossed the dog, That worried the cat, That killed the rat, That ate the malt **That lay in the house that Jack built.**
8 7,8 6,7,8 5,6,7,8 4,5,6,7,8 3,4,5,6,7,8 2,3,4,5,6,7,8 1,2,3,4,5,6,7,8	This is the priest all shaven and shorn, That married the man all tattered and torn, That kissed the maiden all forlorn, That milked the cow with the crumpled horn, That tossed the dog, That worried the cat, That killed the rat, That ate the malt **That lay in the house that Jack built.**
9 8,9 7,8,9 6,7,8,9 5,6,7,8,9 4,5,6,7,8,9 3,4,5,6,7,8,9 2,3,4,5,6,7,8,9 1,2,3,4,5,6,7,8,9	This is the cock that crowed in the morn, That waked the priest all shaven and shorn, That married the man all tattered and torn, That kissed the maiden all forlorn, That milked the cow with the crumpled horn, That tossed the dog, That worried the cat, That killed the rat, That ate the malt **That lay in the house that Jack built.**
10 9,10 8,9,10 7,8,9,10 6,7,8,9,10 5,6,7,8,9,10 4,5,6,7,8,9,10 3,4,5,6,7,8,9,10 2,3,4,5,6,7,8,9,10 1,2,3,4,5,6,7,8,9,10	This is the farmer sowing his corn, That kept the cock that crowed in the morn, That waked the priest all shaven and shorn, That married the man all tattered and torn, That kissed the maiden all forlorn, That milked the cow with the crumpled horn, That tossed the dog, That worried the cat, That killed the rat, That ate the malt **That lay in the house that Jack built.**

4.D **Solo Line Choral Reading**

Class reads while solo reader reads the assigned lines.

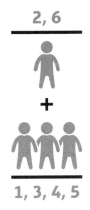

2, 6

+

1, 3, 4, 5

> **Twinkle, Twinkle, Little Star**
> 1. Twinkle, twinkle, little star
> 2. How I wonder what you are
> 3. Up above the world so high
> 4. Like a diamond in the sky
> 5. Twinkle, twinkle, little star
> 6. How I wonder what you are

Fluency Skills Practiced

E
Expression

☐

A
Automatic
Word Recognition

☑

R
Rhythm
and Phrasing

☑

S
Smoothness

☑

Solo line choral reading differs from other forms of choral reading in that some lines are read by just one student. At first, students who are comfortable reading aloud usually volunteer to be the solo reader, but over time, and with repetition of the same text, students who may struggle or be nervous to read aloud will volunteer, too, as they become familiar with the text and the format. They see themselves as successful readers, gaining self-confidence.

Materials Needed	Copy of a Solo Line Choral Reading page projected for all students to view and read (pp. 172–175)
Grades	2–8
Length of Activity	5–10 minutes depending on the length of text
Location	school or home
Extension Idea	• Practice the text in class, then send a copy home so students can practice with an older sibling, partner, or guardian. Require students to read it a certain number of times, then have a parent/guardian sign and return it to class to check off that the homework was completed.

Directions: Read aloud the poem as a class, reading smoothly and in unison. Assign a solo reader to the boldfaced lines.

When You Are Old

by William Butler Yeats

When you are old and grey and full of sleep,
And nodding by the fire, take down this book,
And slowly read, and dream of the soft look
Your eyes had once, and of their shadows deep;

How many loved your moments of glad grace,
And loved your beauty with love false or true,
But one man loved the pilgrim soul in you,
And loved the sorrows of your changing face;

And bending down beside the glowing bars,
Murmur, a little sadly, how Love fled
And paced upon the mountains overhead
And hid his face amid a crowd of stars.

Directions: Read aloud the poem as a class, reading smoothly and in unison. Assign a solo reader to the boldfaced lines.

A Song About Myself

(excerpt)

by **John Keats**

There was a naughty boy,
A naughty boy was he,
He would not stop at home,
He could not quiet be–
He took
In his knapsack
A book
Full of vowels
And a shirt
With some towels,
A slight cap
For night cap,
A hair brush,
Comb ditto,
New stockings
For old ones
Would split O!
This knapsack
Tight at's back
He rivetted close
And followed his nose
To the north,
To the north,
And follow'd his nose
To the north.

Directions: Read aloud the nursery rhyme as a class, reading smoothly and in unison. Assign a solo reader to the boldfaced lines.

London Bridge

London Bridge is falling down
Falling down, falling down
London Bridge is falling down
My fair lady.

Build it up with iron bars
Iron bars, iron bars
Build it up with iron bars
My fair lady.

Iron bars will bend and break
Bend and break, bend and break
Iron bars will bend and break
My fair lady.

Build it up with gold and silver
Gold and silver, gold and silver
Build it up with gold and silver
My fair lady.

London Bridge is falling down
Falling down, falling down
London Bridge is falling down
My fair lady.

Directions: Read or sing the song as a class, reading smoothly and in unison. Assign a solo reader to the boldfaced lines.

Oh My Darling, Clementine

In a cavern, in a canyon,
Excavating for a mine
Dwelt a miner, forty-niner,
And his daughter, Clementine.

Oh my darling, oh my darling,
Oh my darling, Clementine!
Thou art lost and gone forever
Dreadful sorry, Clementine.

Light she was and like a fairy,
And her shoes were number nine,
Herring boxes, without topses,
Sandals were for Clementine.

Oh my darling, oh my darling,
Oh my darling, Clementine!
Thou art lost and gone forever
Dreadful sorry, Clementine.

Drove she ducklings to the water
Ev'ry morning just at nine,
Hit her foot against a splinter,
Fell into the foaming brine.

Oh my darling, oh my darling,
Oh my darling, Clementine!
Thou art lost and gone forever
Dreadful sorry, Clementine.

Ruby lips above the water,
Blowing bubbles, soft and fine,
But, alas, I was no swimmer,
So I lost my Clementine.

Oh my darling, oh my darling,
Oh my darling, Clementine!
Thou art lost and gone forever
Dreadful sorry, Clementine.

How I missed her! How I missed her,
How I missed my Clementine,
But I kissed her little sister,
I forgot my Clementine.

Oh my darling, oh my darling,
Oh my darling, Clementine!
Thou art lost and gone forever
Dreadful sorry, Clementine.

**Fluency Skills
Practiced**

E

Expression

☐

A

Automatic
Word Recognition

☑

R

Rhythm
and Phrasing

☑

S

Smoothness

☑

4.E Call-and-Response Choral Reading

**Two groups: one group does a
"call," the other a "response."**

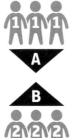

Twinkle, Twinkle, Little Star

A 1. Twinkle, twinkle, little star

B 2. How I wonder what you are

A 3. Up above the world so high

B 4. Like a diamond in the sky

A 5. Twinkle, twinkle, little star

B 6. How I wonder what you are

Students are placed into two groups, one to "call" and the other to "respond," to read a text aloud, with a focus on staying as one voice and reading with rhythm and smoothness.

Materials Needed	Copy of a Call-and-Response Choral Reading page projected for all students to view and read (pp. 177–180)
Grades	2–8
Length of Activity	5–10 minutes depending on the length of text
Location	school or home
Extension Ideas	• Divide students into groups such as girls/boys, kids who prefer fiction/kids who prefer nonfiction, birthdays July and earlier/ birthdays August and later, etc. • Practice the text in class, then send a copy home so students can practice with an older sibling, partner, or guardian. Require students to read it a certain number of times, then have a parent/ guardian sign and return it to class to check off that the homework was completed. • For great poems, check out *Dirty Face* by Shel Silverstein. Here you'll find the title poem: www.poetryfoundation.org/ poems/55343/dirty-face.

Directions: Get into two groups. Choose one group to "call" (C) and one group to "respond" (R) as you read the text. Read boldfaced lines all together.

I Hear America Singing

by Walt Whitman

	I hear America singing, the varied carols I hear,		
C:	Those of mechanics,	R:	each one singing his as it should be blithe and strong,
C:	The carpenter singing	R:	his as he measures his plank or beam,
C:	The mason singing	R:	his as he makes ready for work, or leaves off work,
C:	The boatman singing	R:	what belongs to him in his boat, the deckhand singing on the steamboat deck,
C:	The shoemaker singing	R:	as he sits on his bench, the hatter singing as he stands,
C:	The wood-cutter's song,	R:	the ploughboy's on his way in the morning, or at noon intermission or at sundown,
C:	The delicious	R:	singing of the mother,
C:	or of the young wife	R:	at work,
C:	or of the girl	R:	sewing or washing.

Each singing what belongs to him or her and to none else,
The day what belongs to the day—
at night the party of young fellows, robust, friendly,
Singing with open mouths their strong melodious songs.

Directions: Get into two groups. Choose one group to "call" (C) and one group to "respond" (R) as you read the text.

If

by Rudyard Kipling

C:	If you can keep your head when all about you	R:	Are losing theirs and blaming it on you,
C:	If you can trust yourself when all men doubt you,	R:	But make allowance for their doubting too;
C:	If you can wait and not be tired by waiting,	R:	Or being lied about, don't deal in lies,
C:	Or being hated, don't give way to hating,	R:	And yet don't look too good, nor talk too wise:
C:	If you can dream—and not make dreams your master;	R:	If you can think—and not make thoughts your aim;
C:	If you can meet with Triumph and Disaster	R:	And treat those two impostors just the same;
C:	If you can bear to hear the truth you've spoken	R:	Twisted by knaves to make a trap for fools,
C:	Or watch the things you gave your life to, broken,	R:	And stoop and build 'em up with worn-out tools:
C:	If you can make one heap of all your winnings	R:	And risk it on one turn of pitch-and-toss,
C:	And lose, and start again at your beginnings	R:	And never breathe a word about your loss;
C:	If you can force your heart and nerve and sinew	R:	To serve your turn long after they are gone,
C:	And so hold on when there is nothing in you	R:	Except the Will which says to them: 'Hold on!'
C:	If you can talk with crowds and keep your virtue,	R:	Or walk with Kings—nor lose the common touch,
C:	If neither foes nor loving friends can hurt you,	R:	If all men count with you, but none too much;
C:	If you can fill the unforgiving minute	R:	With sixty seconds' worth of distance run,
C:	Yours is the Earth and everything that's in it,	R:	And—which is more—you'll be a Man, my son!

Directions: Get into two groups. Choose one group to "call" (C) and one group to "respond" (R) as you read the text.

Baa, Baa, Black Sheep

(adaptation)

C:	Baa, baa, *black* sheep, have you any wool?
R:	Yes, sir, yes, sir, three bags full. One for the master, one for the dame, And one for the little boy, who lives down the lane.
C:	Baa, baa, *white* sheep, have you any wool?
R:	Yes, sir, yes, sir, three bags full. One to mend a jumper, one to mend a frock, and one for the little girl, with holes in her sock.
C:	Baa, baa, *grey* sheep, have you any wool?
R:	Yes, sir, yes, sir, three bags full. One for the kitten, one for the cats, and one for the owner, to knit some woolly hats.
C:	Baa, baa, *brown* sheep, have you any wool?
R:	Yes, sir, yes, sir, three bags full. One for the mommy, one for the daddy, and one for the little baby, who lives down the lane.
C:	Baa, baa, *bare* sheep, have you any wool?
R:	No sir, no sir, no bags full. None for the master, none for the dame, and none for the little boy, who lives down the lane.

Directions: Get into two groups. Choose one group to "call" (C) and one group to "respond" (R) as you read the text.

Where Did You Come From, Baby Dear?

(adaptation)
by George MacDonald

C:	Where did you come from, baby dear?	**R:**	Out of the everywhere into here.
C:	Where did you get your eyes so blue?	**R:**	Out of the sky as I came through.
C:	What makes the light in them sparkle and spin?	**R:**	Some of the starry spikes left in.
C:	Where did you get that little tear?	**R:**	I found it waiting when I got here.
C:	What makes your forehead so smooth and high?	**R:**	A soft hand stroked it as I went by.
C:	What makes your cheek like a warm white rose?	**R:**	I saw something better than anyone knows.
C:	Whence that three-cornered smile of bliss?	**R:**	Three angels gave me at once a kiss.
C:	Where did you get this pearly ear?	**R:**	You spoke, and it came out to hear.
C:	Where did you get those arms and hands?	**R:**	Love made itself into hooks and bands.
C:	Feet, whence did you come, you darling things?	**R:**	From the same box as the cherubs' wings.
C:	How did they all just come to be you?	**R:**	You thought about me, and so I grew.
C:	But how did you come to us, you dear?	**R:**	You thought about you, and so I am here.

4.F Simultaneous Choral Reading

Two groups: one group reads the full text, the other repeats a phrase.

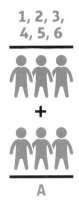

1, 2, 3,
4, 5, 6

+

A

Twinkle, Twinkle, Little Star
1. Twinkle, twinkle, little star
2. How I wonder what you are
3. Up above the world so high
4. Like a diamond in the sky
5. Twinkle, twinkle, little star
6. How I wonder what you are

Phrase
A. Twinkle, twinkle… (repeat)

Fluency Skills Practiced

E
Expression

A
Automatic
Word Recognition

R
Rhythm
and Phrasing

S
Smoothness

Students are placed into two groups, one reading a poem and the other keeping the beat with a repeated phrase from the text. This is different from other forms of reading a poem with two voices: Group A keeps the beat by repeatedly reading a key phrase, while Group B performs the entire text. The result is a symphony of sound and words that can be quite pleasing to the ear.

Materials Needed	Copy of a Simultaneous Choral Reading page projected in class for all students to view and read (pp. 182–183)
Grades	2–8
Length of Activity	5–10 minutes depending on the length of text
Location	school or home
Extension Ideas	• Practice the text in class, then send a copy home so students can practice with an older sibling, partner, or guardian. Require students to read it a certain number of times, then have a parent/guardian sign and return it to class to check off that the homework was completed. • Have students do one voice, then have groups switch and do the opposite voice.

Directions: Divide into two groups. Members of Group A whisper their words in unison while members of Group B simultaneously read the words in chunks as shown, in a rhythm to match Group A.

Twinkle, Twinkle, Little Star

by Jane Taylor

Group A	Group B	Group A	Group B
twinkle, twinkle	Twinkle, twinkle,	twinkle, twinkle	He could not see
twinkle, twinkle	little star,	twinkle, twinkle	which way to go,
twinkle, twinkle	How I wonder	twinkle, twinkle	If you did not
twinkle, twinkle	what you are!	twinkle, twinkle	twinkle so.
twinkle, twinkle	Up above	twinkle, twinkle	In the dark blue
twinkle, twinkle	the world so high,	twinkle, twinkle	sky you keep,
twinkle, twinkle	Like a diamond	twinkle, twinkle	And often through
twinkle, twinkle	in the sky.	twinkle, twinkle	my curtains peep,
twinkle, twinkle	When the blazing	twinkle, twinkle	For you never
twinkle, twinkle	sun is gone,	twinkle, twinkle	shut your eye,
twinkle, twinkle	When he nothing	twinkle, twinkle	Till the sun
twinkle, twinkle	shines upon,	twinkle, twinkle	is in the sky.
twinkle, twinkle	Then you show	twinkle, twinkle	As your bright
twinkle, twinkle	your little light,	twinkle, twinkle	and tiny spark,
twinkle, twinkle	Twinkle, twinkle,	twinkle, twinkle	Lights the traveler
twinkle, twinkle	all the night.	twinkle, twinkle	in the dark,
twinkle, twinkle	Then the traveler	twinkle, twinkle	Though I know
twinkle, twinkle	in the dark,	twinkle, twinkle	not what you are,
twinkle, twinkle	Thanks you for	twinkle, twinkle	Twinkle, twinkle,
twinkle, twinkle	your tiny spark.	twinkle, twinkle	little star.

Directions: Divide into two groups. Members of Group A whisper their words in unison while members of Group B simultaneously read the words in chunks as shown, in a rhythm to match Group A.

The Mulberry Bush

Group A	Group B	Group A	Group B
mulberry bush	Here we go round	paint the fence	This is the way
mulberry bush	the mulberry bush	paint the fence	we paint the fence
mulberry bush	The mulberry bush,	paint the fence	Paint the fence,
mulberry bush	the mulberry bush	paint the fence	paint the fence
mulberry bush	Here we go round	paint the fence	This is the way
mulberry bush	the mulberry bush	paint the fence	we paint the fence
mulberry bush	So early in	paint the fence	So early
mulberry bush	the morning	paint the fence	Thursday morning
bale the hay	This is the way	groom the horse	This is the way
bale the hay	we bale the hay	groom the horse	we groom the horse
bale the hay	Bale the hay,	groom the horse	Groom the horse,
bale the hay	bale the hay	groom the horse	groom the horse
bale the hay	This is the way	groom the horse	This is the way
bale the hay	we bale the hay	groom the horse	we groom the horse
bale the hay	So early	groom the horse	So early
bale the hay	Monday morning	groom the horse	Friday morning
feed the chicks	This is the way	milk the cows	This is the way
feed the chicks	we feed the chicks	milk the cows	we milk the cows
feed the chicks	Feed the chicks,	milk the cows	Milk the cows,
feed the chicks	feed the chicks	milk the cows	milk the cows
feed the chicks	This is the way	milk the cows	This is the way
feed the chicks	we feed the chicks	milk the cows	we milk the cows
feed the chicks	So early	milk the cows	So early
feed the chicks	Tuesday morning	milk the cows	Saturday morning
sweep the porch	This is the way	mulberry bush	Here we go round
sweep the porch	we sweep the porch	mulberry bush	the mulberry bush
sweep the porch	Sweep the porch,	mulberry bush	The mulberry bush,
sweep the porch	sweep the porch	mulberry bush	the mulberry bush
sweep the porch	This is the way	mulberry bush	Here we go round
sweep the porch	we sweep the porch	mulberry bush	the mulberry bush
sweep the porch	So early	mulberry bush	So early
sweep the porch	Wednesday morning	mulberry bush	Sunday morning

**Fluency Skills
Practiced**

E

Expression

☑

A

Automatic
Word Recognition

☑

R

Rhythm
and Phrasing

☑

S

Smoothness

☑

4.G Line-a-Child Choral Reading

**Each student is assigned an individual
line, but a few lines are read together.**

5, 6

Twinkle, Twinkle, Little Star
1. Twinkle, twinkle, little star
2. How I wonder what you are
3. Up above the world so high
4. Like a diamond in the sky

ALL | 5. Twinkle, twinkle, little star
| 6. How I wonder what you are

Each student is assigned one line of the text to read, then practices the line
until he or she can read it smoothly. From there, the poem is read aloud in
its entirety, with each student chiming in at the appropriate point. Everyone
chimes in on the boldfaced lines.

Materials Needed	Copy of a Line-a-Child Choral Reading page projected for all students to view and read (pp. 185–188)
Grades	2–8
Length of Activity	5–10 minutes depending on the length of text
Location	school or home
Extension Ideas	• Practice the poem in class, then send a copy home so students can practice with an older sibling, partner, or guardian. Require students to read it a certain number of times, then have a parent/guardian sign and return it to class to check off that the homework was completed. • Choose poems with lots of short lines. If necessary, partner students to create enough "parts" for everyone. • Once students have read this chorally, give everyone a new number and read again; this can be repeated several times.

Directions: Practice reading aloud your assigned line. Then read the whole poem as a class, with each student reading his or her line solo. Read the boldfaced lines all together.

O Captain! My Captain!

by Walt Whitman

1. O Captain! my Captain! our fearful trip is done,
2. The ship has weather'd every rack, the prize we sought is won,
3. The port is near, the bells I hear, the people all exulting,
4. While follow eyes the steady keel, the vessel grim and daring;

But O heart! heart! heart!

5. O the bleeding drops of red,
6. Where on the deck my Captain lies,
7. Fallen cold and dead.

O Captain! my Captain!

8. Rise up and hear the bells;
9. Rise up—for you the flag is flung—for you the bugle trills,
10. For you bouquets and ribbon'd wreaths—for you the shores a-crowding,
11. For you they call, the swaying mass, their eager faces turning;

Here Captain! dear father!

12. This arm beneath your head!
13. It is some dream that on the deck,
14. You've fallen cold and dead.
15. My Captain does not answer, his lips are pale and still,
16. My father does not feel my arm, he has no pulse nor will,
17. The ship is anchor'd safe and sound, its voyage closed and done,
18. From fearful trip the victor ship comes in with object won;
    Exult O shores, and ring O bells!
19. But I with mournful tread,
20. Walk the deck my Captain lies,

Fallen cold and dead.

Directions: Practice reading aloud your assigned line. Then read the whole poem as a class, with each student reading his or her line solo. Read the boldfaced lines all together.

The Star-Spangled Banner

by Francis Scott Key

O say can you see by the dawn's early light

1. What so proudly we hailed at the twilight's last gleaming?
2. Whose broad stripes and bright stars thru the perilous fight,
3. O'er the ramparts we watched were so gallantly streaming?
4. And the rocket's red glare, the bombs bursting in air,
5. Gave proof through the night that our flag was still there.
6. Oh, say does that star-spangled banner yet wave

O'er the land of the free and the home of the brave?

7. On the shore, dimly seen through the mists of the deep,
8. Where the foe's haughty host in dread silence reposes,
9. What is that which the breeze, o'er the towering steep,
10. As it fitfully blows, half conceals, half discloses?
11. Now it catches the gleam of the morning's first beam,
12. In full glory reflected now shines in the stream:
13. Tis the star-spangled banner! Oh long may it wave

O'er the land of the free and the home of the brave!

14. And where is that band who so vauntingly swore
15. That the havoc of war and the battle's confusion,
16. A home and a country should leave us no more!
17. Their blood has washed out their foul footsteps' pollution.
18. No refuge could save the hireling and slave
19. From the terror of flight, or the gloom of the grave:
20. And the star-spangled banner in triumph doth wave

O'er the land of the free and the home of the brave!

21. O thus be it ever, when freemen shall stand
22. Between their loved home and the war's desolation!
23. Blest with victory and peace, may the heav'n rescued land
24. Praise the Power that hath made and preserved us a nation.
25. Then conquer we must, when our cause it is just,
26. And this be our motto: "In God is our trust."
27. And the star-spangled banner in triumph shall wave

O'er the land of the free and the home of the brave!

Directions: Practice reading aloud your assigned line. Then read the whole poem as a class, with each student reading his or her line solo. Read the boldfaced lines all together.

The Road Not Taken

by Robert Frost

Two roads diverged in a yellow wood,

1. And sorry I could not travel both
2. And be one traveler, long I stood
3. And looked down one as far as I could
4. To where it bent in the undergrowth;
5. Then took the other, as just as fair,
6. And having perhaps the better claim,
7. Because it was grassy and wanted wear;
8. Though as for that the passing there

Had worn them really about the same,

9. And both that morning equally lay
10. In leaves no step had trodden black.
11. Oh, I kept the first for another day!
12. Yet knowing how way leads on to way,
13. I doubted if I should ever come back.
14. I shall be telling this with a sigh
15. Somewhere ages and ages hence:
16. Two roads diverged in a wood, and I—

I took the one less traveled by,
And that has made all the difference.

Directions: Practice reading aloud your assigned line. Then read the whole poem as a class, with each student reading his or her line solo. Read the boldfaced lines all together.

Jabberwocky

by Lewis Carroll

'Twas brillig, and the slithy toves
Did gyre and gimble in the wabe:
All mimsy were the borogoves,
And the mome raths outgrabe.

1. "Beware the Jabberwock, my son!
2. The jaws that bite, the claws that catch!
3. Beware the Jubjub bird, and shun
4. The frumious Bandersnatch!"
5. He took his vorpal sword in hand;
6. Long time the manxome foe he sought—
7. So rested he by the Tumtum tree
8. And stood awhile in thought.
9. And, as in uffish thought he stood,
10. The Jabberwock, with eyes of flame,
11. Came whiffling through the tulgey wood,
12. And burbled as it came!
13. One, two! One, two! And through and through
14. The vorpal blade went snicker-snack!
15. He left it dead, and with its head
16. He went galumphing back.
17. "And hast thou slain the Jabberwock?
18. Come to my arms, my beamish boy!
19. O frabjous day! Callooh! Callay!"
20. He chortled in his joy.

'Twas brillig, and the slithy toves
Did gyre and gimble in the wabe:
All mimsy were the borogoves,
And the mome raths outgrabe.

4.H **Impromptu Choral Reading**

Students individually choose the line they want to read.

> **Twinkle, Twinkle, Little Star**
> 1. Twinkle, twinkle, little star
> 2. How I wonder what you are
> 3. Up above the world so high
> 4. Like a diamond in the sky
> 5. Twinkle, twinkle, little star
> 6. How I wonder what you are

From a poem or song, each student chooses lines he or she wants to read; then the piece is read aloud. Be sure that all lines have been chosen by students before performing the text.

Materials Needed	Copy of an Impromptu Choral Reading page projected for all students to view and read (pp. 190–193)
Grades	2–8
Length of Activity	5–10 minutes depending on the length of text
Location	school or home
Extension Ideas	• Practice the poem in class, then send a copy home so students can practice with an older sibling, partner, or guardian. Require students to read it a certain number of times, then have a parent/guardian sign and return it to class to check off that the homework was completed. • Choose poems with lots of short lines. If necessary, partner students to create enough "parts" for everyone.

Fluency Skills Practiced

E
Expression

A
Automatic Word Recognition

R
Rhythm and Phrasing

S
Smoothness

Directions: Choose particular lines from "You're a Grand Old Flag" you want to sing and then sing the song as a class.

You're a Grand Old Flag

by George M. Cohan

1. You're a grand old flag,
2. You're a high flying flag
3. And forever in peace may you wave.
4. You're the emblem of
5. The land I love.
6. The home of the free and the brave.
7. Ev'ry heart beats true
8. 'neath the Red, White, and Blue,
9. Where there's never a boast or brag.
10. Should auld acquaintance be forgot,
11. Keep your eye on the grand old flag.

> **Directions:** Choose particular lines from "My Shadow" you want to read and then read aloud the poem as a class.

My Shadow

by Robert Louis Stevenson

1 I have a little shadow that goes in and out with me,

2 And what can be the use of him is more than I can see.

3 He is very, very like me from the heels up to the head;

4 And I see him jump before me, when I jump into my bed.

5 The funniest thing about him is the way he likes to grow—

6 Not at all like proper children, which is always very slow;

7 For he sometimes shoots up taller like an India-rubber ball,

8 And he sometimes gets so little that there's none of him at all.

9 He hasn't got a notion of how children ought to play,

10 And can only make a fool of me in every sort of way.

11 He stays so close beside me, he's a coward you can see;

12 I'd think shame to stick to nursie as that shadow sticks to me!

13 One morning, very early, before the sun was up,

14 I rose and found the shining dew on every buttercup;

15 But my lazy little shadow, like an arrant sleepy-head,

16 Had stayed at home behind me and was fast asleep in bed.

> **Directions:** Choose particular lines from "The Brook" you want to read and then read aloud the poem as a class.

The Brook

(excerpt)

by Alfred Tennyson

1   I chatter, chatter, as I flow
2   To join the brimming river,
3   For men may come and men may go,
4   But I go on forever.

5   I wind about, and in and out,
6   With here a blossom sailing,
7   And here and there a lusty trout,
8   And here and there a grayling.

9   I steal by lawns and grassy plots,
10 I slide by hazel covers;
11 I move the sweet forget-me-nots
12 That grow for happy lovers.

13 I slip, I slide, I gloom, I glance,
14 Among my skimming swallows;
15 I make the netted sunbeams dance
16 Against my sandy shallows.

17 I murmur under moon and stars
18 In brambly wildernesses;
19 I linger by my shingly bars;
20 I loiter round my cresses.

21 And out again I curve and flow
22 To join the brimming river;
23 For men may come and men may go,
24 But I go on forever.

Directions: Choose particular lines from "The Violet" you want to read and then read aloud the poem as a class.

The Violet

by Jane Taylor

1   Down in a green and shady bed,
2   A modest violet grew;
3   Its stalk was bent, it hung its head,
4   As if to hide from view.

5   And yet it was a lovely flower,
6   No colours bright and fair;
7   It might have graced a rosy bower,
8   Instead of hiding there.

9   Yet there it was content to bloom,
10   In modest tints arrayed;
11   And there diffused its sweet perfume,
12   Within the silent shade.

13   Then let me to the valley go,
14   This pretty flower to see;
15   That I may also learn to grow
16   In sweet humility.

**Fluency Skills
Practiced**

E

Expression

A

Automatic
Word Recognition

R

Rhythm
and Phrasing

S

Smoothness

4.1 **Echo-Reading**

**Teacher or student reads a
line while class echoes.**

Twinkle, Twinkle, Little Star

A, B 1. Twinkle, twinkle, little star
A, B 2. How I wonder what you are
A, B 3. Up above the world so high
A, B 4. Like a diamond in the sky
A, B 5. Twinkle, twinkle, little star
A, B 6. How I wonder what you are

You or a student read lines of a text, one at a time, as the class "echoes" back the same line (not the next line) to the reader, using the same expression. You can also divide the class into two groups and assign one group "the reader" and the other "the echoer."

Materials Needed	Copy of an Echo-Reading page projected for each student to view and read (pp. 195–198)
Grades	2–8
Length of Activity	5–10 minutes depending on the length of text
Location	school or home
Extension Ideas	• Assign a student the text the night before and have him or her practice reading it; the next day, he or she can be the one that the class "echoes." • Divide students into two groups and have one group echo the other group. • Show students how to vary expression when reading poems, by doing things such as varying volume, intonation, and pausing.

> **Directions:** One person reads the poem. After each line, the class echoes it back to the reader, using the same expression.

Caterpillar

by Christina Rossetti

Brown and furry

Caterpillar in a hurry,

Take your walk

To the shady leaf, or stalk,

Or what not,

Which may be the chosen spot.

No toad spy you,

Hovering bird of prey pass by you;

Spin and die,

To live again a butterfly.

> **Directions:** One person reads the poem. After each line, the class echoes it back to the reader, using the same expression.

At the Sea-Side

by Robert Louis Stevenson

When I was down beside the sea

A wooden spade they gave to me

To dig the sandy shore.

My holes were empty like a cup.

In every hole the sea came up,

Till it could come no more.

Directions: One person reads the poem. After each line, the class echoes it back to the reader, using the same expression.

Whole Duty of Children

by Robert Louis Stevenson

A child should always say what's true,

And speak when he is spoken to,

And behave mannerly at table;

At least as far as he is able.

Directions: One person reads the address. After each line, the class echoes it back to the reader, using the same expression.

Address to Congress

(excerpt)

by Lyndon B. Johnson

This great, rich,
restless country
can offer opportunity
and education and hope to all:
black and white,
North and South,
sharecropper and city dweller.
These are the enemies:
poverty, ignorance, disease.
They are our enemies,
not our fellow man,
not our neighbor.
And these enemies, too,
poverty, disease, and ignorance:
We shall overcome.

4.J Reverse Echo-Reading

Two groups: one group reads a line, the other echoes it.

Twinkle, Twinkle, Little Star

A, B 1. Twinkle, twinkle, little star
A, B 2. How I wonder what you are
A, B 3. Up above the world so high
A, B 4. Like a diamond in the sky
A, B 5. Twinkle, twinkle, little star
A, B 6. How I wonder what you are

The class reads lines of a text chorally, one at a time. Then you or a student "echoes" back the same line (not the next line) to the class, using the same expression.

Materials Needed	Copy of a Reverse Echo-Reading page projected for each student to view and read (pp. 200–203)
Grades	2–8
Length of Activity	5–10 minutes depending on the length of text
Location	school or home
Extension Ideas	• Divide the class in half and have the second group echo exactly how the first group reads it. • Assign the poem the night before so students can go home and practice before reading in class as a group. • Show students how to vary expression when reading poems by doing things such as varying volume, intonation, and pausing.

Fluency Skills Practiced

E
Expression

A
Automatic Word Recognition

R
Rhythm and Phrasing

S
Smoothness

Directions: The class reads the speech chorally, pausing after each line for you or a classmate to echo it back to the class, using the same expression.

I Have a Dream

(excerpt)

by Martin Luther King, Jr.

We have also come
to this hallowed spot
to remind America
of the fierce
urgency of now.
This is no time to
engage in the
luxury of cooling
off or to take
the tranquilizing
drug of gradualism.
Now is the time
to make real
the promises
of democracy.

Directions: The class reads the speech chorally, pausing after each line for you or a classmate to echo it back to the class, using the same expression.

Rain in Summer

(excerpt)

by Henry Wadsworth Longfellow

How beautiful is the rain!

After the dust and heat,

In the broad and fiery street,

In the narrow lane,

How beautiful is the rain!

How it clatters along the roofs,

Like the tramp of hoofs!

How it gushes and struggles out

From the throat of the overflowing spout!

Across the window pane

It pours and pours;

And swift and wide,

With a muddy tide,

Like a river down the gutter roars

The rain, the welcome rain!

Directions: The class reads the speech chorally, pausing after each line for you or a classmate to echo it back to the class, using the same expression.

Will There Really Be a Morning?

by Emily Dickinson

Will there really be a morning?

Is there such a thing as day?

Could I see it from the mountains

If I were as tall as they?

Has it feet like water lilies?

Has it feathers like a bird?

Is it brought from famous countries

Of which I have never heard?

Oh, some scholar! Oh, some sailor!

Oh, some wise man from the skies!

Please to tell a little pilgrim

Where the place called morning lies!

Directions: The class reads the speech chorally, pausing after each line for you or a classmate to echo it back to the class, using the same expression.

A Bird Song

by Christina Rossetti

It's a year almost that I have not seen her:
Oh, last summer green things were greener,
Brambles fewer, the blue sky bluer.

It's surely summer, for there's a swallow:
Come one swallow, his mate will follow,
The bird race quicken and wheel and thicken.

Oh happy swallow whose mate will follow
O'er height, o'er hollow! I'd be a swallow,
To build this weather one nest together.

Videos and
downloadables
are available at
Scholastic.com/
FluencyResources.

CHAPTER 5

Use Partner Texts

"Always stick with your buddy."

—Peggy Rathmann, from *Officer Buckle and Gloria*

In Chapter 4, we positioned reading as a social, or community, act. However, a reader can sometimes get lost in a group. Working with one partner can make for a more intense experience, where the two readers are the stars of their own show and must work with and support one another to make for a meaningful and memorable performance.

In this chapter, we explore various ways students can work with a partner to create a fluent reading. When students work with a partner, they have a natural audience that can provide formative and positive feedback and support. Moreover, when they perform with a partner, they develop a sense of teamwork that is essential to living in and enjoying the social world.

We start with interviews, in which partners interview one another about a topic. Then, we move onto Readers' Theater scripts, in which partners tell a story. Next, we move on to "Who Said It?", in which partners read and perform the same script, but from different perspectives.

Partners need to work together to make sure both of their readings capture the right perspectives. We end the chapter by taking a cue from Paul Fleischman, author of *Joyful Noise*, the Newbery Medal winner, by presenting poems that are meant to be read by two people. Fleischman's title reminds us that reading is a joyful act and becomes more joyful when students are asked to work with a partner to read a text in a fluent and expressive manner. Keep in mind, the texts we present are examples of texts you can find on your own. They can also serve as mentor texts for students to create their own partner texts and ensure joyful reading in your classroom.

Strategies

Fluency Skills Practiced

E
Expression

A
Automatic Word Recognition

R
Rhythm and Phrasing

S
Smoothness

5.A **Situational Expressions**

In small groups sitting in a circle, students pick one "line" and one "emotion" from a cut-up Situational Expressions page (pp. 207–210), and read the line while expressing the emotion they chose. Students then pass their emotion to classmates to their right and read their line again, expressing the new emotion. Repeat as desired.

Materials Needed	Copies of "lines" and "emotions" from Situational Expressions pages for each small group (pp. 207–210)
Grades	2–8
Length of Activity	10–15 minutes
Location	school
Extension Ideas	• Invite students to work in small groups and each come up with one line and one emotion, then follow the same routine; while some lines won't match the emotion well, students will have fun trying to make it work. • After going around in a group, have students lay down all the cards in a central place and decide what phrase goes best with each emotion. Doing this encourages repeated readings of the lines, while carefully considering emotions when reading.

Lines:

"I have school today."

"My mom came to the park."

"The ice cream spilled on my skirt."

"She told me to leave the store."

"I can't find my keys."

"My dog is in the backyard."

Emotions:

scared	excited
anxious	irritated
energetic	confused

Lines:

> "Who told you to come over?"

> "Follow me over here."

> "Why is she calling me?"

> "Come over on Thursday night."

> "How much more do I have to read?"

> "Move just a little to the left."

Emotions:

thrilled	bold
puzzled	caring
calm	lonely

Lines:

"Where did you get that?"
"I can't believe you did that."
"Help me with my painting."
"I don't want to."
"I ran away as quickly as I could."
"I read my book for an hour."

Emotions:

relaxed	jealous
shy	horrified
hurt	aggressive

Lines:

"I have to babysit my brother again."

"I caught the Frisbee three times in a row."

"My new skateboard is bright green."

"How many times do I have to tell you?"

"Throw it to me carefully."

"I wanted to go first."

Emotions:

shocked	annoyed
grateful	suspicious
cautious	playful

5.B **Interviews/Dialogues**

Students read aloud interviews and dialogues in a Readers' Theater format. This is great practice for formal speaking because students must pay special attention to tone and pacing to sound natural, as if they were engaging in a real interview or dialogue.

Materials Needed	Copy of an Interviews/Dialogues page for each student (pp. 212–218)
Grades	2–8
Length of Activity	20 minutes
Location	school or home
Extension Ideas	• Have students research on the Internet and read interviews of other authors. • Encourage students to create a list of questions and then interview family members or friends who live out of town or locally.

Fluency Skills Practiced

E
Expression

A
Automatic Word Recognition

R
Rhythm and Phrasing

S
Smoothness

School Secretary

Directions: With a partner, take on the roles of school secretary and parent. Then practice the dialogue and perform it for an audience.

School Secretary: Good morning, Lincoln School, this is Diane. How may I help you?
Parent: Good morning, this is Marcia Sanderman, Nadia's mother. I'm calling because she's not feeling well today, and I am going to keep her home today.

School Secretary: I'm so sorry to hear that. I hope it's not too bad.
Parent: No, no. She has a slight fever and a cough. Nothing too serious, I hope.

School Secretary: Well, I hope she feels well soon.
Parent: Thank you. Do you think I could get her homework for today?

School Secretary: Is there any specific class?
Parent: I'm especially worried about math and science.

School Secretary: Okay, is it okay for me to give your phone number to Nadia's teachers? They can call you later today with any assignments.
Parent: That would be great. Do you have my phone number on file?

School Secretary: Just a moment. … We have 847-555-2323. Is that correct?
Parent: Yes, that is correct. But I also have a cell number; it's 847-555-3684.

School Secretary: Okay, I'll make sure Mr. Maxwell and Ms. Smith get your message and contact information.
Parent: Thank you very much.

School Secretary: I hope Nadia feels better soon.
Parent: She should be fine by tomorrow. At least that's what I am hoping. Thank you so much for your help.

School Secretary: My pleasure. Have a wonderful day.
Parent: Thank you. Goodbye.

School Secretary: Goodbye.

Sam and Sharon

Directions: With a partner, take on the roles of friends Sam and Sharon. Then practice the dialogue and perform it for an audience.

Background: Two friends in school, having a conversation

Sam: Hi Sharon, what are you working on?
Sharon: Hello Sam. Oh, I'm just studying for our science exam.

Sam: I hate science. I think it's boring.
Sharon: I don't. It's interesting. I'm reading about photosynthesis right now.

Sam: Do you mean people who take pictures?
Sharon: No, silly. How plants make food using the light from the sun.

Sam: Oh. I wonder why I never heard of it before.
Sharon: You are hopeless. So, what are you doing?

Sam: I'm preparing for my club's meeting later today.
Sharon: When's the meeting?

Sam: It's scheduled for 3:30 pm, right after school.
Sharon: … and what are you preparing?

Sam: I'm giving a presentation on our proposal for new school rules.
Sharon: Really?

Sam: Yep. We are going to propose to the principal that homework be reduced to one day a week.
Sharon: That sounds interesting. Do you think Mrs. Shatz will go for it?

Sam: Well, at our meeting, we plan on coming up with reasons why this would be a good rule.
Sharon: Oh, really? Are there good reasons for limiting homework?

Sam: Well, as a matter of fact, there are. For one, kids and parents are stressed too much today, and daily homework just adds to the stress.
Sharon: Hmmm. Interesting. Come up with a few more reasons like that, and I think Mrs. S. will have to give your proposal a lot of thought.

Sam: That's what we're hoping.
Sharon: Well, good luck to you and your club. I'll be pulling for you.

An Interview With Children's Book Author Judy Blume

Directions: With a partner, take on the roles of author Judy Blume and the person interviewing her. Then practice the interview and perform it for an audience. You can shorten the transcript by eliminating some of the questions and answers.

Do you think of the plot first or the characters when you write a story?

I almost always think of characters first.

How do you come up with such great ideas for plots, like in *Tales of a Fourth Grade Nothing?*

I'm really quite bad at coming up with plot ideas. I like to create characters and just see what will happen to them when I let them loose!

What are some suggestions for good character development?

Observe. Make notes. Listen carefully. Listen to how people talk to one another. A good writer is always a people watcher.

Where did you get the idea for the characters Fudge, Peter, and Tootsie?

Fudge is based on my son, Larry, when he was a toddler. A very interesting child. Peter and Tootsie are from my imagination. At least, I think they are.

How did you come up with characters' names in *Freckle Juice* and *Fudge-a-Mania*?

Character names pop into my head. I've no idea where they come from. But since I've written so many books, I sometimes use the phone book for names, too.

Did you want freckles when you were younger, like in *Freckle Juice*?

No, I got the idea for *Freckle Juice* from my daughter, Randy. When she was small, she'd get into the bathtub at night and make a mess. She called this concoction Freckle Juice. It consisted of baby powder, shampoo, and anything else she could mix together. So I had to write a book with that title. That time I had a title first!

Why do you like to write about families?

What else is there? No, really, I like families. I like all the drama about families, and we all come from families, don't we?

What gives you ideas: people, places, things, or all of them?

Ideas seem to come from everywhere—my life, everything I see, hear, and read, and most of all, from my imagination. I have a LOT of imagination.

How do you organize your thoughts before you write a novel? Do you write an outline?

I keep a notebook and jot down everything that comes to mind about characters and places and anything else. That notebook is my security blanket. That way I never feel alone with a blank page or a blank screen.

Do you write your books all at once or in fragments as you get ideas?

I write one scene at a time. I keep a notebook before I start a book with everything I can think of about my characters, so that I'm never totally alone with a blank screen or page. Once I begin a book, I try to sit at my desk for two or three hours every morning.

Did you want to write when you were young?

I never really thought of writing professionally. I never knew it was a possibility. I liked writing in school; I wrote for the school paper. I have always liked to make up stories.

When you first started writing, did you have any doubts about whether you could do it? What kept you going?

I was filled with doubts. At night I would think, I'll never get anything published. But in the morning I'd wake up and say I CAN do this. It's hard to deal with rejection, but if you write, it's a fact of life.

How did you write before there were computers?

I started on my old college typewriter. Then I bought my first electric typewriter when I sold my first book. Then I moved to a computer. But if you want to know the truth, I still get my best ideas scribbling with a pencil.

What is your favorite part of the writing process?

I'm a re-writer. The first draft is torture! It's so hard for me. Once I've written the first draft, I have the pieces to the puzzle, and I love to put it together and make it into a whole. I rewrite about five times. Though with *Summer Sisters*, I went through about 20 drafts!!!

What do you do when you are not writing?

When I'm not writing . . . hmmm . . . well, I kayak in summer and ride my bike in winter (in Key West). I love going to the movies and to the theater and reading. My one regret is that I seem to have less and less time for just sitting and reading! I really miss that time to myself to get lost in a good book.

Did you ever have an author that inspired your writing style?

Oh, yes! I was so inspired by Beverly Cleary's funny and wonderful books. And also, Louise Fitzhugh's *Harriet the Spy*. And E. L. Konigsberg's first book, *Jennifer Hecate*. And my favorite books from when I was young, the Betsy-Tacy books.

What do you think makes a book good?

Well, when I'm reading, I like to care about the characters. I like to know what's inside their heads. And when I'm writing, the same thing is true. For me, character is everything. I'm interested in people and how they cope and how they relate.

Who were your heroes when you were a kid?

That's an interesting question. I think, because I didn't know people with very exciting jobs or careers, my heroes—aside from my father, who was definitely my hero—were movie stars. They seemed to lead exciting lives. Also, I wanted to be a detective.

Were there any teachers or other adults who inspired and encouraged you to become an author?

I had a writing teacher when I was in my twenties and decided to take a course. She encouraged me. At school I had an English teacher, Mr. Komishane, who encouraged and supported all of our creative work. But no one thought I should become a writer. That was my idea, and I didn't get it until I was grown.

What was your favorite childhood book?

I loved *Madeline* when I was very young. Then I loved the Maud Hart Lovelace series about Betsy, Tacy, and Tib. I also liked the Oz series. And Nancy Drew. Basically, I just loved to read. I read whatever I could find. My parents had shelves of books in our living room.

Did you take any special classes before you started writing stories?

I don't think writing classes necessarily help you become a writer, but I did take a course in writing at New York University, which was my alma mater. My teacher there gave me what every writer needs, support and encouragement.

What advice would you give to an aspiring young author?

Keep writing! Don't let anyone ever discourage you. Just keep on going, because you can't help yourself. You have to write! No one chooses to become a writer. You write because you can't not write.

Do you think that your books encourage kids to read?

Well, I hope so. I think any book that someone likes encourages that person to pick up another, and that's how readers are made.

What kinds of books do you like to read?

I like to read fiction. I like to get completely involved in the characters' lives. Sometimes, when I'm writing fiction, I have to switch to reading nonfiction.

Do you celebrate when you finish writing a book?

Oh, yes! But there's also a tremendous letdown. It's as if you have to say good-bye to your best friends, the people you've been so close to for a year or two or three. Some writers get depressed when they finish.

If you could change anything about your writing, what would it be?

That's a hard one to answer. It's best not to dwell on what you've written, wishing it could be different. We all write what we can. We do the very best we can. You might think, oh, I wish I could write like so-and-so, but you have to write like yourself.

What are some editing strategies that you use?

The very best for me is to read aloud, to listen carefully. You'll find you really want to edit as you go. I always tell writers when they've finished a book, put it away. Take it out in a month and read it aloud. A funny story: I was recording one of the Fudge books and as I read I kept changing things and the engineer kept stopping me and saying, "You read that wrong." And I said, "I know, but it's better this way!" But it was too late to edit. I had to read it as it was.

Do you have a special place to go when you get writer's block?

Writer's block, what's that?! There are good days and less good days, but I refuse to acknowledge writer's block. Although, for really good thinking, I do like to go to the water to just sit at the ocean or the pond. I like my kayak for thinking, too. And my bicycle. We all have some days that are better than others. If it's a bad day, if it just won't come, get up and walk around, do something else. Tomorrow it will come.

How do you feel when an editor tells you to change a part of a story that you feel is just fine?

It hasn't worked that way for me. An editor would question something rather than say change it. A good editor can explain why something doesn't work, and sometimes you have to argue your point. You should, if you're really convinced you're on the right track. I've done that a couple of times. Mostly I've had excellent relationships with editors. I need a good editor. Who doesn't? A good editor brings a fresh eye to your manuscript. I would never want to publish without working with a good editor.

Does anyone else in your family write?

My husband, George Cooper, has a nonfiction book coming out this spring—*Poison Widows*. And my daughter, Randy Blume, has a novel coming out called *Crazy in the Cockpit*. I'm a proud wife and mom!

What was your favorite subject when you were in school?

English. Drama. I was always dramatic! My aunt called me Camille.

Did your parents read to you a lot as a child?

It's funny, I don't think my parents read to me very often. But they were book lovers. I read to my children and now to my grandson. He loves being read to at bedtime, even though he's just learned to read. You should never stop reading aloud.

Do people treat you as someone famous or as a regular person?

I can't relate to people who treat me as a "famous person." I only like to hang around with people who treat me as a regular person because that's what I am. All people are really just regular.

As a child, did you daydream a lot? If so, is that where your story ideas come from?

Yes, I was a great daydreamer. You know what I worry about? I worry that kids today don't have enough time to just sit and daydream. I was a great pretender, always making up stories inside my head. Stories and stories and stories, but I never told anyone.

Judy, do you have any final words for the audience?

You've been the most exciting audience with the best questions! Thank you all so much for being here with me. I think you've inspired me. I think I may have to write another book after all.

This Is Your Life

Name: _____   Date: _____

> **Directions**: Complete the interview questions in the spaces below. Then pair up with a classmate, choose your roles (interviewer and student), practice the interview, and perform it for an audience.

Interviewer: Hi there. Please tell us your name and where you are from.

Student:

Interviewer: What would you like people to know about you? Do you have any special talents that you can share with us?

Student:

Interviewer: If you could change one thing about school, what would it be and why?

Student:

Interviewer: When you're finished with school, what would you like to be or do as an adult?

Student:

Interviewer: Thank you very much for speaking with me.

5.C **Proverb Readers' Theater**

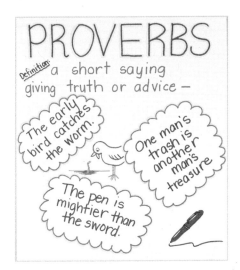

Partners choose parts and practice reading a short, rich Readers' Theater script inspired by a well-known proverb. They should read the script several times, focusing on expression, automaticity, and phrasing.

Materials Needed	Copy of a Proverb Readers' Theater page for each student (pp. 220–222) Pencil for each student
Grades	2–8
Length of Activity	10–15 minutes
Location	school or home
Extension Ideas	• Have students make up their own short Readers' Theater scripts, either orally or written. • Spend time teaching the students what each proverb means, then do research on where it started in the first place. • Ask students to follow up each script with a paragraph about why they think the proverb is true and a situation in their lives when they have experienced something to do with the saying.

Fluency Skills Practiced

E
Expression

A
Automatic
Word Recognition

R
Rhythm
and Phrasing

S
Smoothness

The Early Bird Catches the Worm

Directions: With a partner, choose your part, and practice the script individually and then together. Be sure your expression matches what is happening in the exchange!

Bird:	I fly and stretch and look for you.
Worm:	I wiggle and squirm and watch for you, too.
Bird:	You strut your stuff and look so fat.
Worm:	You fly around to avoid the cat.
Bird:	I must find you and fill my belly.
Worm:	You should leave me alone and go find a deli!
Bird:	But you are my favorite, perfect and gooey.
Worm:	Find someone else to be your chewy-chew-chewy.
Bird:	I will come get you one day soon.
Worm:	Then I will hide from night 'til noon!
Together:	The early bird catches the worm!

What Does the Proverb Mean?
Those who are timely and prepared are usually successful.

The Pen Is Mightier Than the Sword

Directions: With a partner, choose your part, and practice the script individually and then together. Be sure your expression matches what is happening in the exchange!

Pen:	My power lies on the inside, wrapped up in ink.
Sword:	My power lies on the outside, a sharp blade to cut anything.
Pen:	I will always be stronger than you, because my power is limitless.
Sword:	But I can cut you, hurt you, shave you, stab you!
Pen:	Do you know my value? Mine comes from within, where it really matters. My words are my power, and I can unleash anything I need.
Sword:	But I can cut through your power with force that you do not have, because I am strong!
Pen:	I may not be strong, but I can change "strong" to "robust" or "tough" or "strapping" or "durable." Can you change yourself so quickly?
Sword:	No, but I am sharp!
Pen:	I may not be sharp, but I can change "sharp" to "jagged" or "clever" or "pointed."
Sword:	Then you win. It must be true that ….
Together:	The pen is mightier than the sword.

What Does the Proverb Mean?
Words can be used as a weapon to conquer others.

One Man's Trash Is Another Man's Treasure

Directions: With a partner, choose your part, and practice the script individually and then together. Be sure your expression matches what is happening in the exchange!

Trash:	I was thrown away because I broke.
Treasure:	I can put you back together!
Trash:	I was discarded because I got too old.
Treasure:	I can make you new again!
Trash:	I was scrapped because I was useless.
Treasure:	I can use you in a completely different way!
Trash:	I was disposed of because I was dirty and worn.
Treasure:	I can clean you up and make you beautiful again!
Trash:	I was ditched because I had already been used.
Treasure:	I can recycle you and use you again!
Together:	One man's trash is another man's treasure.

What Does the Proverb Mean?
Items that some people consider useless can be valuable to others.

5.D **Short Readers' Theater**

Students partner up with a classmate and decide on their parts in a short dialogue. Individually, they will practice their parts, marking up the script, asking how to pronounce words, and trying to read with expression. When each student is comfortable with his or her part, partners get back together and do a mini performance for themselves!

Materials Needed	Copy of a Short Readers' Theater page for each student (pp. 224–226)
Grades	2–8
Length of Activity	20 minutes
Location	school or home
Extension Ideas	• If all students in class are reading the same script, have them practice all week, then at the end of the week, have them get into two groups based on their similar parts and perform the script as a whole class, similar to a choral reading. • Invite students to take home and practice a reading with their parents. To ensure accountability, have the parents sign the script, and then students can return the next day to show they did their "homework!"

Fluency Skills Practiced

E
Expression

A
Automatic Word Recognition

R
Rhythm and Phrasing

S
Smoothness

Tower of Death

Directions: Choose a partner. Read the script below, and decide who will be Reader 1 and Reader 2. Practice your part on your own, and mark the script in ways that will help you read it with expression. Be sure you know how to pronounce each word. When you're comfortable reading your part, practice reading aloud the whole script with your partner.

Reader 1:	Are you ready to get on the Tower of Death?
Reader 2:	No!
Reader 1:	You promised you would do it this time … you have to do it!
Reader 2:	I know, but now that I see the roller coaster up close, I'm way too scared to do it.
Reader 1:	C'mon, just close your eyes and get on. It will be over in no time.
Reader 2:	I can't believe you are talking me into this. What if I get hurt? What if it's too scary? What if … ?
Reader 1:	You can't live your life by asking "What if?" all the time. Sometimes, you just have to go for it!
Reader 2:	Okay, here we go!
Reader 1:	Buckle up!
Reader 2:	I'm buckled! I'm buckled!
Reader 1:	Woo-hoo! Off we go! This first turn is easy, then it drops down 100 feet, so be ready!
Reader 2:	100 what? How am I going to get … AAAAAHHHHHHHHH!
Reader 1:	(Laughs) Wasn't that fun?
Reader 2:	No! I never want to go on another roller coaster again as long as I … AHHHHHHHHH!
Reader 1:	Oh yes, that was the other drop! Wasn't it fabulous?
Reader 2:	Okay, I have to admit that was fun … but only a little. (heavy breathing)
Reader 1:	Thanks for going with me, even though you didn't want to. It's only fair that you get to pick the next ride. What do you want to do?
Reader 2:	TOWER OF DEATH!
Readers 1 and 2:	Wooo-hooo!

Superpowers

Directions: Choose a partner. Read the script below and decide who will be Reader 1 and Reader 2. Practice your part on your own, and mark the script in ways that will help you read it with expression. Be sure you know how to pronounce each word. When you're comfortable reading your part, practice reading aloud the whole script with your partner.

Reader 1:	Hey there, little brother, what are you playing with?
Reader 2:	I got a new toy today. It's a race car with a lightning bolt on it!
Reader 1:	Wow! Cool! Can I see it?
Reader 2:	No, it's just for people with superpowers, sorry.
Reader 1:	But I have superpowers.
Reader 2:	I've never seen them before, so I don't believe you. What can you do that's a superpower?
Reader 1:	I can see things in the back of my head.
Reader 2:	What? You can? What's behind you, then … but no peeking!
Reader 1:	Well, behind me is _____ (fill in the blank with something behind you).
Reader 2:	Wow! I didn't know you could do that! You really ARE a superhero!
Reader 1:	When you get to be older, you can be one too.
Reader 2:	It's okay, I already have a superpower.
Reader 1:	Oh, what's that?
Reader 2:	Pretending to believe my older brother when he pretends he has a superpower. I can see RIGHT through you, mister!
Reader 1:	(laughs) Okay, okay, you got me. But can I still play with you?
Reader 2:	Sure!

Name: _____   Date: _____

Write Your Own!

Directions: Choose a partner to work with. Together, write a short script with two parts. Then practice and perform the script for the class!

Reader 1:	
Reader 2:	
Reader 1:	
Reader 2:	
Reader 1:	
Reader 2:	
Reader 1:	
Reader 2:	
Reader 1:	
Reader 2:	

5.E **Who Said It?**

Students find a partner and read a script in the voices of the people they're assigned. They should read the script twice, in two different voices.

Materials Needed	Copy of Who Said It? page for each student, or shown on projector (pp. 228–229)
Grades	2–8
Length of Activity	10–15 minutes
Location	school or home
Extension Ideas	• After reading the script twice with the given scenarios, have students come up with another scenario that would fit this same script. Working with partners works best so students can brainstorm ideas together. This requires students to do repeated readings of the passage in order to see if their ideas for the scenario work. • Invite students to write their own scripts with their partners, then read it, Readers' Theater style, to the class. Based on the voice and content, the class has to guess what the scenario is and the role of each partner.

Fluency Skills Practiced

E
Expression

A
Automatic
Word Recognition

R
Rhythm
and Phrasing

S
Smoothness

It's for You

Directions: Find a partner and read the script in the voice of the person you're assigned. Then read the script again in a different pair of voices.

First read:

Person A: a teacher accepting late work

Person B: a student turning in late work

Second read:

Person A: a spy needing spy equipment

Person B: a spy who found spy equipment

Person A:	What is that?
Person B:	Oh, this? Well, it's for you.
Person A:	Me? Why?
Person B:	Because I wanted to.
Person A:	Well, it's too late.
Person B:	Sorry, I couldn't help it.
Person A:	Okay, I understand.

Gone

> **Directions**: Find a partner and read the script in the voice of the person you're assigned. Then read the script again in a different pair of voices.

First read:

Person A: a mom who couldn't find her kindergartner who left home on his bike

Person B: a kindergartner who went on a bike ride without telling his mom and just came home

Second read:

Person A: a young girl

Person B: the young girl's puppy

Person A:	Where have you been?
Person B:	I wanted to go away for a little while because you wouldn't give me a treat!
Person A:	You had me worried sick. Don't ever leave like that again.
Person B:	Sometimes, I need my own time without you when I'm mad.
Person A:	You can't do that! It's not safe. Next time, I won't be so nice.
Person B:	It was still fun. I liked being on my own.
Person A:	Please just tell me next time.

Fluency Skills Practiced

E
Expression

A
Automatic
Word Recognition

R
Rhythm
and Phrasing

S
Smoothness

5.F **Poems for Two Voices**

A student and adult read together a poem for two voices (pp. 231–237), each picking one "side" of it. The lines in the middle should be read in unison by the student and adult.

Materials Needed	Copy of a Poems for Two Voices page for student and adult to share (pp. 231–237)
Grades	2–8
Length of Activity	5–10 minutes
Location	school or home
Extension Ideas	• Switch sides once a poem has been read so the child has a chance to practice both parts of it. • Find more poems for two or more voices in these books: *Big Talk: Poems for Four Voices* by Paul Fleischman *I Am Phoenix: Poems for Two Voices* by Paul Fleischman *Joyful Noise: Poems for Two Voices* by Paul Fleischman *Messing Around on the Monkey Bars* by Betsy Franco *Partner Poems for Building Fluency: Grades 2–4* by Bobbi Katz *Partner Poems for Building Fluency: Grades 4–6* by David L. Harrison, Timothy V. Rasinski and Gay Fawcett *Seeds, Bees, Butterflies, and More!* by Carole Gerber *You Read to Me, I'll Read to You: Very Short Fables to Read Together* by Mary Ann Hoberman *You Read to Me, I'll Read to You: Very Short Fairy Tales to Read Together* by Mary Ann Hoberman *You Read to Me, I'll Read to You: Very Short Stories to Read Together* by Mary Ann Hoberman

Directions: Find a partner and read the poem together, with you reading the lines for one voice and your partner reading the lines for the other.

Brussels Sprouts

by David L. Harrison

Voice 1	Voice 2
What's that green thing?	
	Brussels sprouts.
I don't want no Brussels sprouts.	
	Any.
	Come on, try some Brussels sprouts.
I don't want no Brussels sprouts!	
	Any.
	These are special Brussels sprouts.
I don't want no Brussels sprouts!	
	Any.
	Just one taste of Brussels sprouts.
If I taste these Brussels sprouts,	
then can I have something else?	
	Sure!
Ugh!	
I hate these Brussels sprouts!	
	Here's some yummy cottage cheese, pickled beets, cauliflower,
	lima beans, and chicken liver.
Please pass the Brussels sprouts.	
I don't want no chicken liver.	
	Any.

Directions: Find a partner and read the poem together, with you reading the lines for one voice and your partner reading the lines for the other.

The Groanosaur Test

by David L. Harrison and Terry Bond

Voice 1	Voice 2
What do you call a dinosaur in a hurry?	
	A dino-scurry.
What do you call a dinosaur in a snowstorm?	
	A dino-flurry.
What do you call a dinosaur at a funeral?	
	A dino-bury.
What do you call a dinosaur who likes spicy food?	
	A dino-curry.
What do you call a dinosaur stuck in tar?	
	A dino-tarry.
What do you call a dinosaur pulling a wagon?	
	A dino-lorry.
What do you call a dinosaur who takes this test?	
	A dino-sorry!

Directions: Find a partner and read the poem together, with you reading the lines for one voice and your partner reading the lines for the other.

It's a Lollity Popity Day

by David L. Harrison

Voice 1	Voice 2
It's a lollity popity day	
	It's a lollity popity hide-and-go-seekity day.
It's a lollity popity hide-and-go-seekity read a good bookity day.	
	It's a lollity popity hide-and-go-seekity read a good bookity roll in the grassity day.
It's a lollity popity hide-and-go-seekity read a good bookity roll in the grassity talk with a friendity day.	
	It's a lollity popity hide-and-go-seekity read a good bookity roll in the grassity talk with a friendity sit on a lapity day.
It's a lollity popity hide-and-go-seekity read a good bookity roll in the grassity talk with a friendity sit on a lapity play with your petity day.	
	It's a lollity popity hide-and-go-seekity read a good bookity roll in the grassity talk with a friendity sit on a lapity play with your petity happy-go-luckity day.
Hooray!	Hooray!

Directions: Find a partner and read the poem together, with you reading the lines for one voice and your partner reading the lines for the other.

The Grump

by David L. Harrison

Voice 1	Voice 2
Perfect day!	
	I think not
Warm weather	
	Sticky hot
Smell the flowers	
	Makes me sneeze
Pet a kitty	
	No, I'll wheeze
Feed some birdies	
	Hate their litter
Pat a bunny	
	Nasty critter
Gentle clouds	
	Feels like rain
You're so gloomy	
	You're a pain
So much joy	
	So much rot
I think positive	
	I think not!

Directions: Find a partner and read the poem together, with you reading the lines for one voice and your partner reading the lines for the other.

The Farmer and the Raven

Voice 1	Voice 2
A farmer went trotting upon his gray mare,	
	Bumpety, bumpety, bump!
With his daughter behind him so rosy and fair,	
	Lumpety, lumpety, lump!
A raven cried croak! and they all tumbled down,	
	Bumpety, bumpety, bump!
The mare broke her knees, and the farmer his crown,	
	Lumpety, lumpety, lump!
The mischievous raven flew laughing away,	
	Bumpety, bumpety, bump!
And vowed he would serve them the same the next day,	
	Lumpety, lumpety, lump!

Directions: Find a partner and read the poem together, with you reading the lines for one voice and your partner reading the lines for the other.

If All the Seas Were One Sea

Voice 1	Voice 2
If all the seas were one sea	
	What a great sea that would be!
And if all the trees were one tree,	
	What a great tree that would be!
And if all the axes were one axe,	
	What a great axe that would be!
And if all the men were one man,	
	What a great man he would be!
And if the great man took the great axe,	
	And cut down the great tree,
And let it fall into the great sea,	
	What a splish splash that would be!

Directions: Find a partner and read the poem together, with you reading the lines for one voice and your partner reading the lines for the other. Both of you read the lines in the middle.

The Arrow and the Song

by Henry Wadsworth Longfellow

Voice 1	Voice 2
I shot an arrow into the air,	
	It fell to earth, I knew not where;
For, so swiftly it flew, the sight,	
	Could not follow it in its flight.
I breathed a song into the air,	
	It fell to earth, I knew not where;
For who has sight so keen and strong	
	That it can follow the flight of song?
Long, long afterward, in an oak,	
	I found the arrow, still unbroke:

And the song, from beginning to end,

I found again in the heart of a friend.

CHAPTER 6

Make the Most of
Famous Quotes

Videos and
downloadables
are available at
Scholastic.com/
FluencyResources.

CHAPTER 6

Make the Most of Famous Quotes

"When I read a book I seem to read it with my eyes only, but now and then I come across a passage, perhaps only a phrase, which has a meaning for me, and it becomes part of me."

—**W. Somerset Maugham**

All of us have quotations that we remember. For Tim, it's John F. Kennedy's "Ask not what your country can do for you; ask what you can do for your country," which he first heard as a fifth-grade student and which, for him, marked the beginning of a new and promising era in America. If you think about it, much of our culture is formed and explained through oral language—in speeches, poems, songs, and the like.

Famous lines can be found in a variety of texts, from political speeches to children's books. The important information contained in them, along with their brevity, make them ideal for fluency development. To convey the message well, a reader must use his or her voice to stress the meaning and significance of the words.

In this chapter, we explore various ways that you can make famous lines part of your reading curriculum. We start with simple historical quotes that students reconstruct from individual words and then practice and perform. We move on to popular culture, where students take on the role of actor and perform famous lines from movies. Cherished books we share with children contain memorable lines. Students will have a chance to revisit and perform lines from many of those books. Of course, a study of famous lines would not be complete without including famous lines of "the Bard," William Shakespeare. Although Shakespeare is often thought to be for high school and above, the brevity of the quotations makes them accessible to elementary and middle-school students. We end by going beyond individual lines to have students read, rehearse, and perform excerpts from famous speeches. Not only will students have opportunities to improve their fluency, they will also see how speeches can shape culture.

Fluency doesn't develop overnight. It develops through ongoing exploration of words and reading texts orally and expressively. Working with famous lines shows students that developing fluency can impact the world.

Strategies

**Fluency Skills
Practiced**

E

Expression

A

Automatic
Word Recognition

R

Rhythm
and Phrasing

S

Smoothness

6.A **Scrambled Famous Quotes**

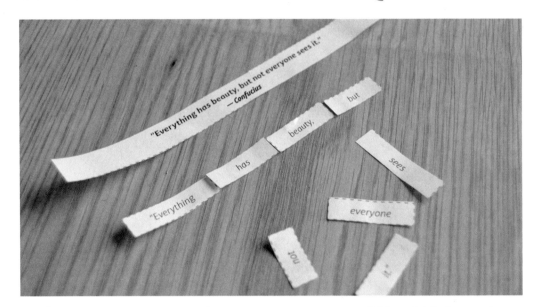

Students reconstruct cut-up famous quotes on pages 241 to 246. Cut each quote apart and, if you choose, laminate the individual word cards. Then have partners try to figure out the quote by moving the cards around. Once partners have unscrambled the quote, ask them to practice reading it with expression, discuss its meaning, and share their quote and thoughts about it with the class. This exposes students to words of wisdom, and gets them thinking about sentence syntax.

Materials Needed	Copies of quotes from the Scrambled Famous Quotes pages, cut up into individual words and scrambled (pp. 241–246).
Grades	2–8 (Choose quotes appropriate for your grade level.)
Length of Activity	10–15 minutes
Location	school or home
Extension Ideas	• Do this activity with the whole class, in small groups, in pairs, individually, or as part of a literacy center. • Have students write about the quote's meaning, giving examples and situations where the quote may prove to be true.

"If you can't stand the heat, get out of the kitchen."
— Harry S. Truman

"If	you	can't	stand	the	heat,
get	out	of	the	kitchen."	

"Keep your friends close and your enemies closer."
— Sun Tzu

"Keep	your	friends	close	and	your
enemies	closer."				

"When one door closes, another opens."
— Alexander Graham Bell

"When	one	door	closes,	another	opens."

"A thing of beauty is a joy forever."
— John Keats

"A	thing	of	beauty	is	a
joy	forever."				

"Beauty is in the eye of the beholder."
— Margaret Hungerford

"Beauty	is	in	the	eye	of
the	beholder."				

"Everything has beauty, but not everyone sees it."
— Confucius

"Everything	has	beauty,	but	not	everyone
sees	it."				

"Spread love everywhere you go."
— Mother Teresa

"Spread	love	everywhere	you	go."

"We need not wait to see what others do."
— Mahatma Gandhi

"We	need	not	wait	to	see
what	others	do."			

"The only thing constant in life is change."
— François de la Rochefoucauld

"The	only	thing	constant	in	life
is	change."				

"A friend is one who knows all about you and likes you anyway."
— Elbert Hubbard

"A	friend	is one	who	knows	all
about	you	and	likes	you	anyway."

"Leave nothing for tomorrow which can be done today."
— Abraham Lincoln

"Leave	nothing	for	tomorrow	which	can
be	done	today."			

"Winners never quit and quitters never win."
— Vince Lombardi

"Winners	never	quit	and	quitters	never
win."					

"Failure is only the opportunity more intelligently to begin again."
— Henry Ford

"Failure	is	only	the	opportunity	more
intelligently	to	begin	again."		

"Many receive advice, only the wise profit from it."
— Publilius Syrus

"Many	receive	advice,	only	the	wise
profit	from	it."			

"Never leave that till tomorrow which you can do today."
— Benjamin Franklin

"Never	leave	that	till	tomorrow	which
you	can	do	today."		

"You can do anything, but not everything."
— David Allen

"You	can	do	anything,	but	not

everything."

"When you're through changing, you're through."
— Martha Stewart

"When	you're	through	changing,	you're	through."

"That which does not kill us makes us stronger."
— Friedrich Nietzsche

"That	which	does	not	kill	us

makes	us	stronger."

"No one can make you feel inferior without your consent."
— Eleanor Roosevelt

"No	one	can	make	you	feel

inferior	without	your	consent."

"Whether you think you can or think you can't, you're right."
— Henry Ford

"Whether	you	think	you	can	or

think	you	can't,	you're	right."

"Early to bed and early to rise, makes a man healthy, wealthy, and wise."
— Benjamin Franklin

| "Early | to bed | and | early | to | rise, |
| makes a | man | healthy, | wealthy, | and | wise." |

"We must learn to live together as brothers or … perish together as fools."
— Martin Luther King, Jr.

| "We | must | learn | to live | together | as |
| brothers | or | perish | together | as | fools." |

"Genius is one percent inspiration and ninety-nine percent perspiration."
— Thomas Alva Edison

| "Genius | is | one | percent | inspiration | and |
| ninety- | nine | percent | perspiration." | | |

"The only thing we have to fear is fear itself."
— Franklin D. Roosevelt

| "The | only | thing | we | have | to |
| fear | is | fear | itself." | | |

"Whatever the mind can conceive and believe, the mind can achieve."
— Napoleon Hill

| "Whatever | the | mind | can | conceive | and |
| believe, | the | mind | can | achieve." | |

"A picture is worth a thousand words."
— Fred R. Barnard

"A	picture	is	worth	a	thousand
words."					

"An eye for an eye only ends up making the whole world blind."
— Mahatma Gandhi

"An	eye	for	an	eye	only
ends up	making	the	whole	world	blind."

"It's not whether you get knocked down, it's whether you get up."
— Vince Lombardi

"It's	not	whether	you	get	knocked
down,	it's	whether	you	get	up."

"The time to repair the roof is when the sun is shining."
— John F. Kennedy

"The	time	to	repair	the	roof
is	when	the	sun	is	shining."

"When you come to the end of your rope, tie a knot and hang on."
— Franklin D. Roosevelt

"When	you	come	to the	end of	your
rope,	tie a	knot	and	hang	on."

"Nothing is particularly hard if you divide it into small jobs."
— Henry Ford

"Nothing	is	particularly	hard	if	you
divide	it	into	small	jobs."	

6.B Famous Lines From Movies

Copy and cut out each movie line on pages 248 to 250, and give one to each student. Students practice reading each line silently and decide how to deliver it with expression, based on the content. Then they practice reading the line with a partner and, when they're ready, deliver it in front of the class.

Materials Needed	Copy of one Famous Movie Line for each student (pp. 248–250)
Grades	2–8 (Choose lines appropriate for your grade level.)
Length of Activity	10–15 minutes
Location	school
Extension Idea	• Have students practice with expression favorite lines from movies they have seen and then share them with the class. Classmates can guess which movie they are from.

Fluency Skills Practiced

E
Expression

A
Automatic
Word Recognition

R
Rhythm
and Phrasing

S
Smoothness

Famous Movie Line 1:

"… Bond. James Bond."

— *Dr. No,* **1962**

Famous Movie Line 2:

"Some people without brains do an awful lot of talking, don't you think?"

— *The Wizard of Oz,* **1939**

Famous Movie Line 3:

"My mama always said, 'Life was like a box of chocolates; you never know what you're gonna get."

— *Forrest Gump,* **1994**

Famous Movie Line 4:

"Always let your conscience be your guide."

— *Pinocchio,* **1940**

Famous Movie Line 5:

"Magic Mirror on the wall, who is the fairest one of all?"

— *Snow White and the Seven Dwarfs,* **1937**

Famous Movie Line 6:

"Carpe diem. Seize the day, boys."

— *Dead Poets Society,* **1989**

Famous Movie Line 7:

"Toto, I have a feeling we're not in Kansas anymore."

— *The Wizard of Oz,* **1939**

Famous Movie Line 8:

"To infinity and beyond!"

— *Toy Story,* **1995**

Famous Movie Line 9:

"May the odds be ever in your favor."

— *The Hunger Games,* **2012**

Famous Movie Line 10:

"Love means never having to say you're sorry."

— *Love Story,* **1970**

Famous Movie Line 11:

"There's no place like home."

— *The Wizard of Oz*, 1939

Famous Movie Line 12:

"Please, sir, I want some more."

— *Oliver!*, 1968

Famous Movie Line 13:

"Ahhhhhhh! I made my family disappear!"

— *Home Alone*, 1990

Famous Movie Line 14:

"I see dead people."

— *The Sixth Sense*, 1999

Famous Movie Line 15:

"Houston, we have a problem."

— *Apollo 13*, 1995

Famous Movie Line 16:

"Life moves pretty fast. If you don't stop and look around once in a while, you could miss it."

— *Ferris Bueller's Day Off*, 1986

Famous Movie Line 17:

"Elementary, my dear Watson."

— *The Adventures of Sherlock Holmes*, 1939

Famous Movie Line 18:

"I'm the king of the world!"

— *Titanic*, 1997

Famous Movie Line 19:

"Here's lookin' at you, kid."

— *Casablanca*, 1941

Famous Movie Line 20:

"It's alive! It's alive!"

— *Frankenstein*, 1931

Famous Movie Line 21:

"If you build it, he will come."

— *Field of Dreams*, 1989

Famous Movie Line 22:

"There's no crying in baseball!"

— *A League of Their Own*, 1992

Famous Movie Line 23:

"You could be happy here, I could take care of you. I wouldn't let anybody hurt you. We could grow up together, E.T."

— *E.T.*, 1982

Famous Movie Line 24:

"Look, Daddy. Teacher says, 'Every time a bell rings, an angel gets his wings!'"

— *It's a Wonderful Life*, 1946

Famous Movie Line 25:

"I'll get you, my pretty, and your little dog, too."

— *The Wizard of Oz*, 1939

Famous Movie Line 26:

"No matter how your heart is grieving, if you keep on believing, the dream that you wish will come true."

— *Cinderella*, 1950

Famous Movie Line 27:

"If you can't say something nice, don't say nothin' at all."

— *Bambi*, 1942

Famous Movie Line 28:

"The past can hurt. But the way I see it, you can either run from it, or learn from it."

— *The Lion King*, 1994

Famous Movie Line 29:

"The answer is only important if you ask the right question."

— *The Next Karate Kid*, 1994

Famous Movie Line 30:

"The flower that blooms in adversity is the most rare and beautiful of all."

— *Mulan*, 1998

6.C **Famous First Lines From Children's Books**

THE BOY WHO LIVED

Mr. and Mrs. Dursley, of number four, Privet Drive, were to say that they were perfectly normal, thank you very n ey were the last people you'd expect to be involved in a strange or mysterious, because they just didn't hold with ense.

Mr. he director of a firm called Grunnings, which

Copy and cut out each famous first line on pages 252 to 255, and give one to each student. Students practice reading the line silently and decide how to deliver it with expression, based on the content. They then practice reading the line with a partner and, when they're ready, deliver it in front of the class.

Materials Needed	Copy of one Famous First Lines From Children's Books page for each student (pp. 252–255)
Grades	2–8 (Choose lines appropriate for your grade level.)
Length of Activity	10–15 minutes
Location	school
Extension Ideas	• Have older students not only read aloud the lines, but also guess the books from which the lines come. • Have students research great first lines—or any lines, for that matter—from books they've read or are reading, and share what makes them so great.

Fluency Skills Practiced

E
Expression

A
Automatic
Word Recognition

R
Rhythm
and Phrasing

S
Smoothness

Famous First Lines From Children's Books 1:

"All children, except one, grow up."

— *Peter Pan* by J. M. Barrie

Famous First Lines From Children's Books 2:

"The sun did not shine, it was too wet to play, so we sat in the house all that cold, cold wet day."

— *The Cat in the Hat* by Dr. Seuss

Famous First Lines From Children's Books 3:

"The first place that I can well remember was a large pleasant meadow with a pond of clear water in it."

— *Black Beauty* by Anna Sewell

Famous First Lines From Children's Books 4:

"Chug, chug, chug. Puff, puff, puff. Ding-dong, ding-dong."

— *The Little Engine That Could* by Watty Piper

Famous First Lines From Children's Books 5:

"'Where's Papa going with that axe?' said Fern to her mother as they were setting the table for breakfast."

— *Charlotte's Web* by E.B. White

Famous First Lines From Children's Books 6:

"When Mary Lennox was sent to Misselthwaite Manor to live with her uncle everybody said she was the most disagreeable-looking child ever seen."

— *The Secret Garden* by Frances Hodgson Burnett

Famous First Lines From Children's Books 7:

"'Christmas won't be Christmas without any presents,' grumbled Jo, lying on the rug."

— *Little Women* by Louisa May Alcott

Famous First Lines From Children's Books 8:

"September. Tuesday. First of all, let me get something straight: This is a JOURNAL, not a diary."

— *Diary of a Wimpy Kid* by Jeff Kinney

Famous First Lines From Children's Books 9:

"Mr. and Mrs. Dursley, of number four Privet Drive, were proud to say that they were perfectly normal, thank you very much."

— *Harry Potter and the Sorcerer's Stone* by J. K. Rowling

Famous First Lines From Children's Books 10:

"When I stepped out into the bright sunlight from the darkness of the movie house, I had only two things on my mind: Paul Newman and a ride home."
— *The Outsiders* **by S. E. Hinton**

Famous First Lines From Children's Books 11:

"Marley was dead, to begin with."
— *A Christmas Carol* **by Charles Dickens**

Famous First Lines From Children's Books 12:

"The year that Buttercup was born, the most beautiful woman in the world was a French scullery maid named Annette."
— *The Princess Bride* **by William Goldman**

Famous First Lines From Children's Books 13:

"We moved on the Tuesday before Labor Day. I knew what the weather was like the second I got up. I knew because I caught my mother sniffing under her arms."
— *Are You There God? It's Me, Margaret* **by Judy Blume**

Famous First Lines From Children's Books 14:

"It's a funny thing about mothers and fathers. Even when their own child is the most disgusting little blister you could ever imagine, they still think that he or she is wonderful."
— *Matilda* **by Roald Dahl**

Famous First Lines From Children's Books 15:

"If you are interested in stories with happy endings, you would be better off reading some other book."
— *The Bad Beginning* **by Lemony Snicket**

Famous First Lines From Children's Books 16:

"Not every 13-year-old girl is accused of murder, brought to trial, and found guilty."
— *The True Confessions of Charlotte Doyle* **by Avi**

Famous First Lines From Children's Books 17:

"The Herdmans were absolutely the worst kids in the history of the world."
— *The Best Christmas Pageant Ever* **by Barbara Robinson**

Famous First Lines From Children's Books 18:

"Ba-room, ba-room, ba-room, baripity, baripity, baripity, baripity—Good."
— *Bridge to Terabithia* **by Katherine Paterson**

Famous First Lines From Children's Books 19:

"Mr. and Mrs. Mallard were looking for a place to live."
— *Make Way for Ducklings* by Robert McCloskey

Famous First Lines From Children's Books 20:

"If you asked the kids and the teachers at Lincoln Elementary School to make three lists—all the really bad kids, all the really smart kids, and all the really good kids—Nick Allen would not be on any of them."
— *Frindle* by Andrew Clements

Famous First Lines From Children's Books 21:

"Alice was beginning to get very tired of sitting by her sister on the bank, and of having nothing to do: once or twice she had peeped into the book her sister was reading, but it had no pictures or conversations in it, 'and what is the use of a book,' thought Alice, 'without pictures or conversation?'"
— *Alice in Wonderland* by Lewis Carroll

Famous First Lines From Children's Books 22:

"In an old house in Paris that was covered with vines lived twelve little girls in two straight lines."
— *Madeline by* Ludwig Bemelmans

Famous First Lines From Children's Books 23:

"The Mole had been working very hard all the morning, spring-cleaning his little home."
— *The Wind in the Willows* by Kenneth Grahame

Famous First Lines From Children's Books 24:

"Most motorcars are conglomerations (this is a long word for bundles) of steel and wire and rubber and plastic, and electricity and oil and gasoline and water, and the toffee papers you pushed down the crack in the back seat last Sunday."
— *Chitty-Chitty-Bang-Bang* by Ian Fleming

Famous First Lines From Children's Books 25:

"It was seven o'clock of a very warm evening in the Seeonee hills when Father Wolf woke up from his day's rest, scratched himself, yawned, and spread out his paws one after the other to get rid of the sleepy feeling in their tips."
— *The Jungle Book* by Rudyard Kipling

Famous First Lines From Children's Books 26:

"Once there were four children whose names were Peter, Susan, Edmund, and Lucy."
— *The Lion, the Witch and the Wardrobe* by C. S. Lewis

Famous First Lines From Children's Books 27:

"It was an afternoon in late September. In the pleasant city of Stillwater, Mr. Popper, the house painter, was going home from work."

— *Mr. Popper's Penguins* by Richard and Florence Atwater

Famous First Lines From Children's Books 28:

"Once on a dark winter's day, when the yellow fog hung so thick and heavy in the streets of London that the lamps were lighted and the shop windows blazed with gas as they do at night, an odd-looking little girl sat in a cab with her father and was driven rather slowly through the big thoroughfares."

— *A Little Princess* by Frances Hodgson Burnett

Famous First Lines From Children's Books 29:

"My name is India Opal Buloni, and last summer my daddy, the preacher, sent me to the store for a box of macaroni-and-cheese, some white rice, and two tomatoes and I came back with a dog."

— *Because of Winn-Dixie* by Kate DiCamillo

Famous First Lines From Children's Books 30:

"Mr. and Mrs. Brown first met Paddington on a railway platform. In fact, that was how he came to have such an unusual name for a bear, for Paddington was the name of the station."

— *Paddington Bear* by Michael Bond

**Fluency Skills
Practiced**

E

Expression

☑

A

Automatic
Word Recognition

☐

R

Rhythm
and Phrasing

☑

S

Smoothness

☐

6.D **Shakespeare's Best**

Copy and cut out each Shakespeare quote on pages 257 to 259, and give one to each student. Students practice reading the quote silently and decide how to deliver it with expression, based on the content. They then practice reading the quote with a partner and, when they're ready, deliver it in front of the class.

Materials Needed	Copy of one of Shakespeare's Best for each student (pp. 257–259)
Grades	5–8 (Choose quotes appropriate for your grade level.)
Length of Activity	10–15 minutes
Location	school
Extension Idea	• Before they perform, have students research on the Internet what the quote means and why it was said in the literary work. This will help them understand the context and know how to use expression best.

Shakespeare's Best 1:

"To be, or not to be: that is the question."

— *Hamlet*

Shakespeare's Best 2:

"All the world's a stage, and all the men and women merely players. They have their exits and their entrances; And one man in his time plays many parts."

— *As You Like It*

Shakespeare's Best 3:

"Romeo, Romeo, wherefore art thou Romeo?"

— *Romeo and Juliet*

Shakespeare's Best 4:

"Some are born great, some achieve greatness, and some have greatness thrust upon them."

— *Twelfth Night*

Shakespeare's Best 5:

"What's in a name? A rose by any other name would smell as sweet."

— *Romeo and Juliet*

Shakespeare's Best 6:

"Uneasy lies the head that wears a crown."

— *Henry IV*

Shakespeare's Best 7:

"I am a man more sinned against than sinning."

— *King Lear*

Shakespeare's Best 8:

"What light through yonder window breaks."

— *Romeo and Juliet*

Shakespeare's Best 9:

"Cowards die many times before their deaths; the valiant never taste of death but once."

— *Julius Caesar*

Shakespeare's Best 10:

"Brevity is the soul of wit."

— *Hamlet*

Shakespeare's Best 11:

"Shall I compare thee to a summer's day?"

— "Sonnet 18"

Shakespeare's Best 12:

"To thine own self be true."

— *Hamlet*

Shakespeare's Best 13:

"We know what we are, but know not what we may be."

— *Hamlet*

Shakespeare's Best 14:

"A man can die but once."

— *Henry IV*

Shakespeare's Best 15:

"Full fathom five thy father lies, of his bones are coral made. Those are pearls that were his eyes. Nothing of him that doth fade, but doth suffer a sea-change into something rich and strange."

— *The Tempest*

Shakespeare's Best 16:

"We have seen better days."

— *Timon of Athens*

Shakespeare's Best 17:

"How sharper than a serpent's tooth it is to have a thankless child!"

— *King Lear*

Shakespeare's Best 18:

"The lady doth protest too much, methinks."

— *Hamlet*

Shakespeare's Best 19:

"All that glisters is not gold."

— *The Merchant of Venice*

Shakespeare's Best 20:

"Lord, what fools these mortals be!"

— *A Midsummer Night's Dream*

Shakespeare's Best 21:

"We are such stuff as dreams are made on, and our little life is rounded with a sleep."

— *The Tempest*

Shakespeare's Best 22:

"But, for mine own part, it was Greek to me."

— *Julius Caesar*

Shakespeare's Best 23:

"There is nothing either good or bad, but thinking makes it so."

— *Hamlet*

Shakespeare's Best 24:

"Life's but a walking shadow, a poor player, that struts and frets his hour upon the stage, and then is heard no more; it is a tale told by an idiot, full of sound and fury, signifying nothing."

— *Macbeth*

Shakespeare's Best 25:

"Nothing will come of nothing."

— *King Lear*

Shakespeare's Best 26:

"If you prick us, do we not bleed? If you tickle us, do we not laugh? If you poison us, do we not die? And if you wrong us, shall we not revenge?"

— *The Merchant of Venice*

Shakespeare's Best 27:

"Love looks not with the eyes, but with the mind; and therefore is winged Cupid painted blind."

— *A Midsummer Night's Dream*

Shakespeare's Best 28:

"If music be the food of love, play on."

— *Twelfth Night*

Shakespeare's Best 29:

"The course of true love never did run smooth."

— *A Midsummer Night's Dream*

Shakespeare's Best 30:

"Then must you speak of one who loved not wisely but too well."

— *Othello*

**Fluency Skills
Practiced**

E

Expression

☑

A

Automatic
Word Recognition

☑

R

Rhythm
and Phrasing

☑

S

Smoothness

☑

6.E **Historical Fluency, Famous Speeches**

Students practice reading aloud excerpts from famous speeches from American history.

Materials Needed	Copy of one Historical Fluency, Famous Speeches page for each student (pp. 261–267)
Grades	4–8 (Choose speeches appropriate for your grade level.)
Length of Activity	20 minutes
Location	school or home
Extension Ideas	• Have students take home and deliver the speech to their parents. • Have students research the historical context of the speech, or information about the person who originally made the speech, and why he or she made it.

Directions: Practice reading Patrick Henry's speech with expression. Then perform it in front of the class, or take it home to perform for someone there.

Give Me Liberty or Give Me Death!

(excerpt)

by Patrick Henry
1775

It is natural to man to indulge in the illusions of hope. We are apt to shut our eyes against a painful truth—and listen to the song of that siren, till she transforms us into beasts. Is this the part of wise men, engaged in a great and arduous struggle for liberty? Are we disposed to be of the number of those, who having eyes, see not, and having ears, hear not, the things which so nearly concern their temporal salvation? For my part, whatever anguish of spirit it may cost, I am willing to know the whole truth; to know the worst, and to provide for it.…

…Gentlemen may cry, peace, peace—but there is no peace. The war is actually begun! The next gale that sweeps from the north will bring to our ears the clash of resounding arms! Our brethren are already in the field! Why stand we here idle? What is it that gentlemen wish? What would they have? Is life so dear, or peace so sweet, as to be purchased at the price of chains and slavery? Forbid it, Almighty God!—I know not what course others may take; but as for me, give me liberty or give me death!

Directions: Practice reading Sojourner Truth's speech with expression. Then perform it in front of the class, or take it home to perform for someone there.

Ain't I a Woman

(excerpt)

by Sojourner Truth
1851

Well, children, where there is so much racket there must be something out of kilter. I think that 'twixt the negroes of the South and the women at the North, all talking about rights, the white men will be in a fix pretty soon. But what's all this here talking about?

That man over there says that women need to be helped into carriages, and lifted over ditches, and to have the best place everywhere. Nobody ever helps me into carriages, or over mud-puddles, or gives me any best place! And ain't I a woman? Look at me! Look at my arm! I have ploughed and planted, and gathered into barns, and no man could head me! And ain't I a woman? I could work as much and eat as much as a man—when I could get it—and bear the lash as well! And ain't I a woman? I have borne thirteen children, and seen most all sold off to slavery, and when I cried out with my mother's grief, none but Jesus heard me! And ain't I a woman?

Directions: Practice reading Susan B. Anthony's speech with expression. Then perform it in front of the class, or take it home to perform for someone there.

Women's Rights to the Suffrage

(excerpt)

by Susan B. Anthony
1873

It was we, the people; not we, the white male citizens; nor yet we, the male citizens; but we, the whole people, who formed the Union. And we formed it, not to give the blessings of liberty, but to secure them; not to the half of ourselves and the half of our posterity, but to the whole people—women as well as men. And it is a downright mockery to talk to women of their enjoyment of the blessings of liberty while they are denied the use of the only means of securing them provided by this democratic-republican government—the ballot.

Directions: Practice reading Franklin Roosevelt's address with expression. Then perform it in front of the class, or take it home to perform for someone there.

First Inaugural Address

(excerpt)

by Franklin Delano Roosevelt
1933

So, first of all, let me assert my firm belief that the only thing we have to fear is fear itself—nameless, unreasoning, unjustified terror which paralyzes needed efforts to convert retreat into advance. In every dark hour of our national life, a leadership of frankness and of vigor has met with that understanding and support of the people themselves which is essential to victory. And I am convinced that you will again give that support to leadership in these critical days.

Directions: Practice reading Douglas MacArthur's address with expression. Then perform it in front of the class, or take it home to perform for someone there.

Address to the Corps of Cadets at the West Point Military Academy

(excerpt)

by Douglas MacArthur
1962

You are the leaven, which binds together the entire fabric of our national system of defense. From your ranks come the great captains who hold the nation's destiny in their hands the moment the war tocsin sounds. The Long Gray Line has never failed us. Were you to do so, a million ghosts in olive drab, in brown khaki, in blue and gray, would rise from their white crosses thundering those magic words: Duty, Honor, Country.

This does not mean that you are war mongers.

On the contrary, the soldier, above all other people, prays for peace, for he must suffer and bear the deepest wounds and scars of war.

But always in our ears ring the ominous words of Plato, that wisest of all philosophers: "Only the dead have seen the end of war."

The shadows are lengthening for me. The twilight is here. My days of old have vanished, tone and tint. They have gone glimmering through the dreams of things that were. Their memory is one of wondrous beauty, watered by tears, and coaxed and caressed by the smiles of yesterday. I listen vainly, but with thirsty ears, for the witching melody of faint bugles blowing reveille, of far drums beating the long roll. In my dreams I hear again the crash of guns, the rattle of musketry, the strange, mournful mutter of the battlefield.

But in the evening of my memory, always I come back to West Point.

Always there echoes and re-echoes: Duty, Honor, Country.

Directions: Practice reading Martin Luther King, Jr.'s speech with expression. Then perform it in front of the class, or take it home to perform for someone there.

I Have a Dream

(excerpt)

by Martin Luther King, Jr.
1963

I have a dream that one day this nation will rise up and live out the true meaning of its creed: "We hold these truths to be self-evident, that all men are created equal."

I have a dream that one day on the red hills of Georgia, the sons of former slaves and the sons of former slave owners will be able to sit down together at the table of brotherhood.

I have a dream that one day even the state of Mississippi, a state sweltering with the heat of injustice, sweltering with the heat of oppression, will be transformed into an oasis of freedom and justice.

I have a dream that my four little children will one day live in a nation where they will not be judged by the color of their skin but by the content of their character.

I have a dream today!

Directions: Practice reading Barbara Jordan's speech with expression. Then perform it in front of the class, or take it home to perform for someone there.

Keynote Speech at the Democratic National Convention

(excerpt)

by Barbara Jordan
1976

We are a people in a quandary about the present. We are a people in search of our future. We are a people in search of a national community. We are a people trying not only to solve the problems of the present, unemployment, inflation, but we are attempting on a larger scale to fulfill the promise of America. We are attempting to fulfill our national purpose, to create and sustain a society in which all of us are equal.

CHAPTER 7

Create a Literate
Environment
Where Fluency
Can Flourish

Videos and
downloadables
are available at
**Scholastic.com/
FluencyResources.**

CHAPTER 7

Create a Literate Environment Where Fluency Can Flourish

"I think a major act of leadership... is to create the places and processes so people can actually learn together..."

—Margaret J. Wheatley

In the college literacy classes we teach, we often ask students if there is a place where and a time when they most enjoy reading. Most students indicate that they do have preferences. For some it is reading on the patio on a warm summer's day, with soft music and a cool drink. For others it's in a warm bed in the evening, after a long day of work. And still others have told us that when they read for academic or business reasons, rather than for pleasure, they find it best to sit in a straight-back chair at a table, in a quiet space.

Reading is indeed "Length and Location" oriented. Some reading is best done in some places, and other reading is best done in other places. In this chapter, we share ideas for creating environments that are conducive to focusing on and engaging in fluent reading.

The whole-class teacher read-aloud is at the top of our list. We know that children who are read to get a model of fluent reading by the teacher and are more likely to develop comprehension and vocabulary skills. But there is more to read-aloud than picking up a book and reading it to the class. Listening centers provide places where students can listen to recorded texts read in a fluent manner. Buddy reading, like read-aloud, seems easy enough—pair up students and have them read together for 10 to 15 minutes. However, advance planning can maximize the benefit of buddy reading. Poetry, by its very nature, is meant to be performed. Is it possible to create the types of poetry performances for both the classroom and our communities? We say yes. Similarly, Readers' Theater works best when it's part of a special classroom event for which students perform their scripts. We call these Readers' Theater Festivals. Finally, "I Have… Who Has…?" is an interactive process in which students learn about, read, and perform various forms of figurative language.

Creating environments in which students want to work on fluency will pay dividends in moving them not only to more fluent reading, but also to a greater love of words and reading in general.

Strategies

**Fluency Skills
Practiced**

E

Expression

A

Automatic
Word Recognition

R

Rhythm
and Phrasing

S

Smoothness

✓

7.A **Read-Aloud**

Students listen to you read a story or other type of text with fluency.

- Prepare for the read-aloud by reviewing the text in advance and deciding how you will read it.

- Read to students in an audible and expressive voice. Stop occasionally to discuss what you are reading and to model critical thinking or inferring.

- After the read-aloud, discuss the text. Be sure to discuss how you used your voice to make the reading more enjoyable and meaningful for them. Return to the text and reread especially fluent parts, and invite students to share how your expression affected their listening.

Materials Needed	A book to read aloud, chosen by you
Grades	1–8
Length of Activity	10–15 minutes
Location	school or home
Extension Ideas	• Make read-aloud a regular and consistent part of the school day so students can anticipate it. • Create a comfortable environment. For example, you can sit in a rocking chair and invite students to sit on the floor.

7.B **Listening Center**

Students learn to read a text fluently by repeatedly listening to an audio-recorded version of a text, while reading a print version of it. During their center time, assign students a text that they will be asked to read independently later. Tell students that one way to learn to read a text is to listen to an audio-recorded version of it while following along in the print version. Do this several times until students feel that they are able to read the text independently, without relying on the audio-recorded version.

Fluency Skills Practiced

E
Expression

A
Automatic
Word Recognition

R
Rhythm
and Phrasing

S
Smoothness

Materials Needed	Collections of book chapters, poems, scripts, and other texts that have a fluent audio-recorded version
Grades	2–8
Length of Activity	15–20 minutes
Location	school or home
Extension Ideas	• Create your own audio-recorded versions of texts. Chapters from stories, poems, and Readers' Theater scripts work particularly well. Online applications are available that allow you to record texts electronically (e.g., www.audacityteam.org). • Allow students to visit the listening center daily. It can be made part of the regular literacy curriculum. • Have students add to the listening center collection by recording their own fluent readings of texts.

**Fluency Skills
Practiced**

E

Expression

A

Automatic
Word Recognition

R

Rhythm
and Phrasing

S

Smoothness

7.C **Buddy Reading**

Your class partners up with a younger or older class, and each of your students is assigned a buddy to read with. The older student can read the text first. Then, if necessary, the younger student can read it with help from the older student.

Materials Needed	A text that is leveled for younger readers
Grades	2–8
Length of Activity	20–30 minutes
Location	school
Extension Ideas	• See Kid Tips for Buddy Reading With Younger Kids: How Do I Keep Their Attention? (p. 273) • See Teacher Tips for Buddy Reading With Younger Kids: How Do I Organize and Manage Buddy Reading? (p. 274)

Kid Tips for Buddy Reading With Younger Kids

How Do I Keep Their Attention?

- Keep young kids entertained by reading with a lot of expression.

- Make sound effects throughout the book to match what you are reading. If there is a train, make a "toot toot" sound. Or, if there is a monster, make a monster sound.

- Tell them they can ask questions during the book. Then stop and answer questions when they have them.

- Read slowly so they catch all the words.

- Stop and ask them questions about the book as you go, such as, "Where is the brown dog?" and "Why is the dog sad?" Or have them point to things on the page and talk about them.

- At the end, ask them their favorite part, and have them find it in the book and tell why it was their favorite.

Teacher Tips for Buddy Reading With Younger Kids

How Do I Organize and Manage Buddy Reading?

- Put kids in groups of four instead of two, so if someone is absent, everyone still has a partner or group.

- Instruct older students how to act and read with younger children. Use the "Kid Tips for Buddy Reading With Younger Kids" to help.

- Have the older children practice reading the book several times before they read to the younger kids. They should sound fluent in their reading to keep the younger students' attention.

- Spend some time at the beginning letting the kids get to know each other. Have an activity planned that will help kids with this.

- Allow kids to sit where they want. The younger kids can even bring a pillow the day of buddy reading to find a cozy spot to read in the classroom with their buddy/buddies.

7.D **Poetry Jam**

Students fluently read and perform a chosen poem to classmates and other audience members.

- At the beginning of the week, assign to individual or small groups of students a poem to perform at an end-of-week Poetry Jam.

- Each week's Poetry Jam can focus on a theme (e.g., spring, hope) or a particular poet (e.g., Langston Hughes, Bruce Lansky).

- Throughout the week, give students opportunities to rehearse their assigned poems. You may want to read the poems to students to model fluent reading of them.

- On the last day of the week, allow 30 minutes for the jam. Dim the lights and bring in a bar stool for readers to sit on. Readers should strive to convey the meaning and mood of the poem.

- After each reading, be sure audience members applaud the performer(s) and offer positive comments about their reading.

Materials Needed	A poem chosen by the student or teacher How to Read a Poem sheet (p. 276)
Grades	2–8
Length of Activity	30 minutes
Location	school
Extension Idea	• Use the How to Read a Poem sheet to help students learn strategies for reading a poem with meaning.

Fluency Skills Practiced

E

Expression

A

Automatic Word Recognition

R

Rhythm and Phrasing

S

Smoothness

How to Read a Poem

- Look at the poem's title. What might this poem be about?

- Read the poem aloud without trying to understand it.

- Read it again for understanding. Start with what you know. Underline the parts you do not understand.

- Clarify the meaning of unfamiliar words.

- Look for patterns. Watch for repeated, interesting, or unfamiliar use of language, imagery, sound, color, or arrangement. What might the poet be trying to do with these patterns?

- Look for changes within the poem—in tone, focus, narrator, structure, voice, or patterns. What has changed and what does the change mean?

- Who is speaking in the poem? What does the poem tell you about him or her?

- Know what the poem means so you know where to use expression.

Poetry Reading Strategies

Preview the poem by reading the title and paying attention to the poem's form (shape on the page, stanzas, number of lines, and ending punctuation).

Read the poem aloud several times to hear rhyme, rhythm, and the overall sound of the poem. This makes it easier to understand the poem.

Visualize the images by paying close attention to strong verbs and comparisons in the poem. Do the images remind you of anything? Let the comparisons paint a picture in your head.

Clarify words and phrases by allowing yourself to find the meaning of words or phrases that stand out, or are repeated. If you do not understand the meaning, use a dictionary, use context clues, or ask a teacher or peer.

Evaluate the poem's theme by asking what message the poet is trying to send. Does it relate to your life in any way?

7.E **Writing a Poem for Two Voices**

Fluency Skills Practiced

E
Expression

A
Automatic Word Recognition

R
Rhythm and Phrasing

S
Smoothness

Give student partners two poems. Partners then create a new poem for two voices using only words, phrases, or lines from the original poems. Encourage students to be creative. For example, urge them to repeat a word or change around the words in a line. Once students complete their poems and practice reciting them, they can perform them in front of the class.

Materials Needed	Two original poems by authors such as Shel Silverstein and Douglas Florian
Grades	2–8
Length of Activity	30–60 minutes
Location	school or home
Extension Ideas	• Give students two very different poems, which will likely make the new poem much more interesting. For example, a classic poem by Edgar Allan Poe and a silly poem by Shel Silverstein will require students to find a new purpose for and meaning to the words when creating their own poem. • Use two poems by the same poet as part of an author study. Students have to think deeply about the meaning of the poet's words and phrases in order to reuse them in a poem.

**Fluency Skills
Practiced**

E

Expression

A

Automatic
Word Recognition

R

Rhythm
and Phrasing

S

Smoothness

7.F Poetry Flash Mob

Students learn parts of a poem, just as participants in a flash mob learn parts of a dance. They will then surprise their audience by reading or reciting a poem aloud at an unexpected time and place. It's important to choose a location where an audience is guaranteed. One student starts the poem, and then slowly, line by line, other students chime in. The reading ends with all students participating. Longer poems are best for flash mobs, and they are sometimes more easily done when students memorize the poem, but reading the poem can work just as well.

Materials Needed	Any poem that contains many lines
Grades	2–8
Length of Activity	1 week for preparation and presentation
Location	school
Extension Idea	• Have students perform the poem in the classroom and videotape it. Then show a videotape in the school news, or post it on a school or district social media site for the community to see.

7.G Readers' Theater Festival

In small groups, at the end of each week, students perform a Readers' Theater script for an audience of classmates and others that was assigned to them at the beginning of the week.

- At the beginning of the week, assign students to small groups or let them choose their groups. Give each group a script to perform at the end of the week in a Readers' Theater Festival.

- Throughout the week, give students opportunities to rehearse the script and coach each other. You might also read the scripts to students to model fluent reading.

- On the last day of the week, provide 30 to 45 minutes for the weekly festival. Dim the lights and invite each group up, one by one, to perform the script that was assigned at the beginning of the week. Performers should strive to convey the meaning of the script.

- After each reading, encourage audience members to applaud the performance and offer positive comments about it.

Materials Needed	Readers' Theater scripts chosen by you. Many websites offer scripts. Two of our favorites are: www.thebestclass.org/rtscripts.html www.teachingheart.net/readerstheater.htm
Grades	2–8
Length of Activity	1 week for preparation and presentation
Location	school

Fluency Skills Practiced

E
Expression

A
Automatic Word Recognition

R
Rhythm and Phrasing

S
Smoothness

**Fluency Skills
Practiced**

E

Expression

☑

A

Automatic
Word Recognition

☑

R

Rhythm
and Phrasing

☑

S

Smoothness

☑

7.H I Have... Who Has...?

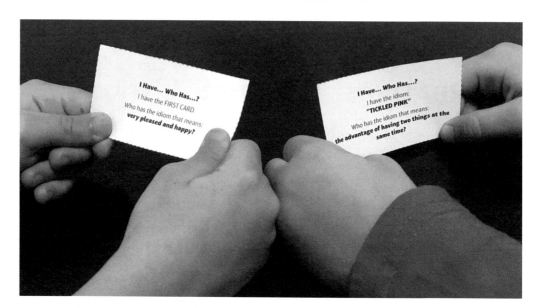

Copy and cut apart the cards (pages 281 to 284), from the Idioms set, the Onomatopoeia set (pages 286 to 288), or the Rhyming Names set (pages 290 to 293). Then give each student one of the cards. (In some instances, you may need to give students two cards because all cards in a set must be used.) The student with "FIRST CARD" begins and reads his or her card, which contains a hint about the idiom, onomatopoeia, or rhyming word. Then the student with the card that matches the "FIRST CARD" reads his or her card, and the student with the card that matches responds. Every card in a set is connected to a card before it and a card after it, until the last card. You can help students make matches by using the answer key provided at the end of each card set.

Materials Needed	Copy of one idiom, onomatopoeia, or rhyming names I Have... Who Has...? card for each student (pp. 281–297)
Grades	2–8
Length of Activity	10 minutes
Location	school
Extension Idea	• Have students do a quick round of one set of cards and then switch to a different one for a fun challenge and to stretch the activity. Be sure to encourage students to listen to the beat and the rhythm of the card they read as well as the cards being read.

I Have... Who Has...? Idioms

I Have... Who Has...?

I have the **FIRST CARD.**

Who has the idiom that means:
very pleased and happy?

I Have... Who Has...?

I have the idiom:
"TICKLED PINK"

Who has the idiom that means:
the advantage of having two things at the same time?

I Have... Who Has...?

I have the idiom:
"BEST OF BOTH WORLDS"

Who has the idiom that means:
being undecided about something?

I Have... Who Has...?

I have the idiom:
"ON THE FENCE"

Who has the idiom that means:
very caring and kind?

I Have... Who Has...?

I have the idiom:
"HEART OF GOLD"

Who has the idiom that means:
a terrible situation based on more than one event?

I Have... Who Has...?

I have the idiom:
"PERFECT STORM"

Who has the idiom that means:
doing something to make other people feel more comfortable?

I Have... Who Has...?

I have the idiom:
"BREAK THE ICE"

Who has the idiom that means:
something that just barely gets done in time?

I Have... Who Has...?

I have the idiom:
"BY THE SKIN OF YOUR TEETH"

Who has the idiom that means:
something that is very expensive?

I Have... Who Has...?

I have the idiom:
"COSTS AN ARM AND A LEG"

Who has the idiom that means:
describing something that someone is not very good at?

I Have... Who Has...?

I have the idiom:
"DON'T GIVE UP YOUR DAY JOB"

Who has the idiom that means:
a really good idea or invention?

I Have... Who Has...?

I have the idiom:
"THE BEST THING SINCE SLICED BREAD"

Who has the idiom that means:
deciding to take a risk?

I Have... Who Has...?

I have the idiom:
"THROWING CAUTION TO THE WIND"

Who has the idiom that means:
a child that is just like his father or mother?

I Have... Who Has...?

I have the idiom:
"CHIP OFF THE OLD BLOCK"

Who has the idiom that means:
being sick?

I Have... Who Has...?

I have the idiom:
"UNDER THE WEATHER"

Who has the idiom that means:
ignoring someone perhaps because you are mad at them?

I Have... Who Has...?

I have the idiom:
"GIVING SOMEONE THE COLD SHOULDER"

Who has the idiom that means:
someone deciding or being told to stop working on something?

I Have... Who Has...?

I have the idiom:
"CALL IT A DAY"

Who has the idiom that means:
to look everywhere for something or an answer you are searching for?

I Have... Who Has...?

I have the idiom:
"LEAVE NO STONE UNTURNED"

Who has the idiom that means:
feeling very joyful about something?

I Have... Who Has...?

I have the idiom:
"ON CLOUD NINE"

Who has the idiom that means:
someone criticizing someone else even though they might be just as bad about the same thing?

I Have... Who Has...?

I have the idiom:
"THE POT CALLING THE KETTLE BLACK"

Who has the idiom that means:
to make a special effort to do something?

I Have... Who Has...?

I have the idiom:
"GO THE EXTRA MILE"

Who has the idiom that means:
to do something that nobody would expect?

I Have... Who Has...?

I have the idiom:
"PULL A RABBIT OUT OF A HAT"

Who has the idiom that means:
to start something all over again because the first idea didn't work?

I Have... Who Has...?

I have the idiom:
"GO BACK TO THE DRAWING BOARD"

Who has the idiom that means:
to do something that seems pointless and just wastes time?

I Have... Who Has...?

I have the idiom:
"GO ON A WILD GOOSE CHASE"

Who has the idiom that means:
to take on a task or work that is too much to do?

I Have... Who Has...?

I have the idiom:
"BITE OFF MORE THAN YOU CAN CHEW"

Who has the idiom that means:
the idea that you shouldn't complain about something that happened in the past?

I Have... Who Has...?

I have the idiom:
"DON'T CRY OVER SPILT MILK"

Who has the idiom that means:
hearing gossip or a rumor about someone or something?

I Have... Who Has...?

I have the idiom:
"HEAR IT THROUGH THE GRAPEVINE"

Who has the idiom that means:
when someone misses their chance to do something?

I Have... Who Has...?

I have the idiom:
"MISS THE BOAT"

Who has the idiom that means:
taking credit for or ruining the excitement for someone else when they have done something well?

I Have... Who Has...?

I have the idiom:
"STEAL THEIR THUNDER"

Who has the idiom that means:
something that is really easy?

I Have... Who Has...?

I have the idiom:
"PIECE OF CAKE"

Who has the idiom that means:
to give away a secret?

I Have... Who Has...?

I have the idiom:
"LET THE CAT OUT OF THE BAG"

Who has the idiom that means:
something that hardly ever happens?

I Have... Who Has...?

I have the idiom:
"ONCE IN A BLUE MOON"

Who has the idiom that means:
something that is your own decision?

I Have... Who Has...?

I have the idiom:
"THE BALL IS IN YOUR COURT"

Who has the **FIRST CARD?**

I Have... Who Has...? Idioms Answer Key

	I have the idiom: "_____"	Who has the idiom that means:
1	I have the FIRST CARD.	very pleased and happy
2	tickled pink	the advantage of having two things at the same time
3	best of both worlds	being undecided about something
4	on the fence	very caring and kind
5	heart of gold	a terrible situation based on more than one event
6	perfect storm	doing something to make other people feel more comfortable
7	break the ice	something that just barely gets done in time
8	by the skin of your teeth	something that is very expensive
9	costs an arm and a leg	describing something that someone is not very good at
10	don't give up your day job	a really good idea or invention
11	the best thing since sliced bread	deciding to take a risk
12	throwing caution to the wind	a child that is just like his father or mother
13	chip off the old block	being sick
14	under the weather	ignoring someone perhaps because you are mad at them
15	giving someone the cold shoulder	someone deciding or being told to stop working on something
16	call it a day	to look everywhere for something or an answer you are searching for
17	leave no stone unturned	feeling very joyful about something
18	on cloud nine	someone criticizing someone else even though they might be just as bad about the same thing
19	the pot calling the kettle black	to make a special effort to do something
20	go the extra mile	to do something that nobody would expect
21	pull a rabbit out of a hat	to start something all over again because the first idea didn't work
22	go back to the drawing board	to do something that seems pointless and just wastes time?
23	go on a wild goose chase	to take on a task or work that is too much to do
24	bite off more than you can chew	the idea that you shouldn't complain over something that happened in the past
25	don't cry over spilt milk	hearing gossip or a rumor about someone or something
26	hear it through the grapevine	when someone misses their chance to do something
27	miss the boat	taking credit for or ruining the excitement for someone else when they have done something well
28	steal their thunder	something that is really easy
29	piece of cake	to give away a secret
30	let the cat out of the bag	something that hardly ever happens
31	once in a blue moon	something that is your own decision
32	the ball is in your court	Who has the FIRST CARD?

I Have… Who Has…? Onomatopoeia

I Have… Who Has…?

I have the **FIRST CARD.**

Who has the onomatopoeia that is the sound:
a clock makes?

I Have… Who Has…?

I have the onomatopoeia:
"TICK-TOCK"

Who has the onomatopoeia that is the sound:
a firecracker makes?

I Have… Who Has…?

I have the onomatopoeia:
"POP"

Who has the onomatopoeia that is the sound:
cymbals make in a band?

I Have… Who Has…?

I have the onomatopoeia:
"CRASH"

Who has the onomatopoeia that is the sound:
of a cannon going off?

I Have… Who Has…?

I have the onomatopoeia:
"BOOM"

Who has the onomatopoeia that is the sound:
when you run into a wall?

I Have… Who Has…?

I have the onomatopoeia:
"WHAM"

Who has the onomatopoeia that is the sound:
a bee makes?

I Have… Who Has…?

I have the onomatopoeia:
"BUZZ"

Who has the onomatopoeia that is the sound:
a cow makes?

I Have… Who Has…?

I have the onomatopoeia:
"MOO"

Who has the onomatopoeia that is the sound:
people make when they drink?

I Have… Who Has…?

I have the onomatopoeia:
"SLURP"

Who has the onomatopoeia that is the sound:
a jack-in-the-box makes?

I Have… Who Has…?

I have the onomatopoeia:
"BOING"

Who has the onomatopoeia that is the sound:
of getting hit in the head with a ball?

I Have... Who Has...?

I have the onomatopoeia:
"BOINK"

Who has the onomatopoeia that is the sound:
of biting into hard food?

I Have... Who Has...?

I have the onomatopoeia:
"CRUNCH"

Who has the onomatopoeia that is the sound:
an ambulance makes?

I Have... Who Has...?

I have the onomatopoeia:
"WOO-OOO"

Who has the onomatopoeia that is the sound:
of a faucet dripping?

I Have... Who Has...?

I have the onomatopoeia:
"DRIP"

Who has the onomatopoeia that is the sound:
of someone sleeping?

I Have... Who Has...?

I have the onomatopoeia:
"ZZZZZ"

Who has the onomatopoeia that is the sound:
of jumping in a puddle?

I Have... Who Has...?

I have the onomatopoeia:
"SPLOSH"

Who has the onomatopoeia that is the sound:
of jumping into a pool?

I Have... Who Has...?

I have the onomatopoeia:
"SPLASH"

Who has the onomatopoeia that is the sound:
of a bomb going off?

I Have... Who Has...?

I have the onomatopoeia:
"KABOOM"

Who has the onomatopoeia that is the sound:
of a telephone alerting you someone is calling?

I Have... Who Has...?

I have the onomatopoeia:
"RING"

Who has the onomatopoeia that is the sound:
you make after eating?

I Have... Who Has...?

I have the onomatopoeia:
"BURP"

Who has the onomatopoeia that is the sound:
you make if you are scared?

I Have... Who Has...?

I have the onomatopoeia:
"SHRIEK"

Who has the onomatopoeia that is the sound:
you make when you put your hands together?

I Have... Who Has...?

I have the onomatopoeia:
"CLAP"

Who has the onomatopoeia that is the sound:
of dropping coins in a metal container?

I Have... Who Has...?

I have the onomatopoeia:
"CLINK"

Who has the onomatopoeia that is the sound:
of a horn honking?

I Have... Who Has...?

I have the onomatopoeia:
"BEEP BEEP"

Who has the onomatopoeia that is the sound:
of a doorbell ringing?

I Have... Who Has...?

I have the onomatopoeia:
"CHIME"

Who has the onomatopoeia that is the sound:
of the ball going in a basket?

I Have... Who Has...?

I have the onomatopoeia:
"SWOOSH"

Who has the onomatopoeia that is the sound:
of making music with your mouth closed?

I Have... Who Has...?

I have the onomatopoeia:
"HUM"

Who has the onomatopoeia that is the sound:
an owl makes?

I Have... Who Has...?

I have the onomatopoeia:
"HOOT"

Who has the onomatopoeia that is the sound:
a snake makes?

I Have... Who Has...?

I have the onomatopoeia:
"HISS"

Who has the onomatopoeia that is the sound:
of something being dropped on the floor above you?

I Have... Who Has...?

I have the onomatopoeia:
"THUMP"

Who has the onomatopoeia that is the sound:
your nose makes when you inhale?

I Have... Who Has...?

I have the onomatopoeia:
"SNORT"

Who has the onomatopoeia that is the sound:
of banging on two round instruments?

I Have... Who Has...?

I have the onomatopoeia:
"DRUM"

Who has the **FIRST CARD?**

I Have... Who Has...? Onomatopoeia Answer Key

	I have the onomatopoeia: "_____"	Who has the onomatopoeia that is the sound:
1	I have the FIRST CARD.	a clock makes
2	tick-tock	a firecracker makes
3	pop	cymbals make in a band
4	crash	of a cannon going off
5	boom	when you run into a wall
6	wham	a bee makes
7	buzz	a cow makes
8	moo	people make when they drink
9	slurp	a jack-in-the-box makes
10	boing	of getting hit in the head with a ball
11	boink	of biting into hard food
12	crunch	an ambulance makes
13	woo-ooo	of a faucet dripping
14	drip	of someone sleeping
15	zzzzz	of jumping in a puddle
16	splosh	of jumping into a pool
17	splash	of a bomb going off
18	kaboom	of a telephone alerting you someone is calling
19	ring	you make after eating
20	burp	you make if you are scared
21	shriek	you make when you put your hands together
22	clap	of dropping coins in a metal container
23	clink	of a horn honking
24	beep beep	of a doorbell ringing
25	chime	of the ball going in a basket
26	swoosh	of making music with your mouth closed
27	hum	an owl makes
28	hoot	a snake makes
29	hiss	of something being dropped on the floor above you
30	thump	your nose makes when you inhale
31	snort	of banging on two round instruments
32	drum	Who has the FIRST CARD?

I Have... Who Has...? Rhyming Names

I Have... Who Has...?

I have the **FIRST CARD.**

Who has the rhyming word for this name?
**My name is Bob.
My favorite food is corn on the_____.**

I Have... Who Has...?

I have the word:
"COB"

Who has the rhyming word for this name?
**My name is Jan.
I ride around town in my _____.**

I Have... Who Has...?

I have the word:
"VAN"

Who has the rhyming word for this name?
**My name is Billy.
In class I always act _____.**

I Have... Who Has...?

I have the word:
"SILLY"

Who has the rhyming word for this name?
**My name is Jack.
After school I have a _____.**

I Have... Who Has...?

I have the word:
"SNACK"

Who has the rhyming word for this name?
**My name is Peter.
When I'm cold I turn on the _____.**

I Have... Who Has...?

I have the word:
"HEATER"

Who has the rhyming word for this name?
**My name is Dan.
I cook bacon in a _____.**

I Have... Who Has...?

I have the word:
"PAN"

Who has the rhyming word for this name?
**My name is Mike.
Before breakfast I like to ride my _____.**

I Have... Who Has...?

I have the word:
"BIKE"

Who has the rhyming word for this name?
**My name is Gary.
My pet dog is really _____.**

I Have... Who Has...?

I have the word:
"HAIRY"

Who has the rhyming word for this name?
My name is Anna.
My favorite fruit is a _____.

I Have... Who Has...?

I have the word:
"BANANA"

Who has the rhyming word for this name?
My name is Drew.
I feel sick because I have the _____.

I Have... Who Has...?

I have the word:
"FLU"

Who has the rhyming word for this name?
My name is Josh.
Even though I hate it, my mom makes me eat
_____.

I Have... Who Has...?

I have the word:
"SQUASH"

Who has the rhyming word for this name?
My name is Scott.
I spilled on my shirt so I have a _____.

I Have... Who Has...?

I have the word:
"SPOT"

Who has the rhyming word for this name?
My name is Doug.
I like a warm _____.

I Have... Who Has...?

I have the word:
"HUG"

Who has the rhyming word for this name?
My name is Nancy.
My sparkle pants are really _____.

I Have... Who Has...?

I have the word:
"FANCY"

Who has the rhyming word for this name?
My name is Matt.
During class I like to _____.

I Have... Who Has...?

I have the word:
"CHAT"

Who has the rhyming word for this name?
My name is Mary.
I like to drink anything that is _____.

I Have... Who Has...?

I have the word:
"DAIRY"

Who has the rhyming word for this name?
My name is Frank.
I've never been in a shark _____.

I Have... Who Has...?

I have the word:
"TANK"

Who has the rhyming word for this name?
My name is Amy.
My brother always likes to _____.

I Have... Who Has...?

I have the word:
"BLAME ME"

Who has the rhyming word for this name?
My name is Pam.
I like to listen to a _____.

I Have... Who Has...?

I have the word:
"JAM"

Who has the rhyming word for this name?
My name is Jean.
My favorite color is lime _____.

I Have... Who Has...?

I have the word:
"GREEN"

Who has the rhyming word for this name?
My name is Carrie.
My family lives on the _____.

I Have... Who Has...?

I have the word:
"PRAIRIE"

Who has the rhyming word for this name?
My name is Jen.
I don't go to bed until _____.

I Have... Who Has...?

I have the word:
"TEN"

Who has the rhyming word for this name?
My name is Tom.
In high school I will go to _____.

I Have... Who Has...?

I have the word:
"PROM"

Who has the rhyming word for this name?
My name is Ken.
Sometimes I chase around my pet _____.

I Have... Who Has...?

I have the word:
"HEN"

Who has the rhyming word for this name?
My name is Rose.
When I see a camera, I always _____.

I Have... Who Has...?

I have the word:
"POSE"

Who has the rhyming word for this name?
My name is Judy.
Sometimes I'm cranky and really _____.

I Have... Who Has...?

I have the word:
"MOODY"

Who has the rhyming word for this name?
My name is Fred.
I dislike going to _____.

I Have... Who Has...?

I have the word:
"BED"

Who has the rhyming word for this name?
My name is Lori.
At night before bed I like to hear a _____.

I Have... Who Has...?

I have the word:
"STORY"

Who has the rhyming word for this name?
My name is Jane.
I'm really smart and use my _____.

I Have... Who Has...?

I have the word:
"BRAIN"

Who has the rhyming word for this name?
My name is Steve.
When I tell a bad joke, my friends say to _____.

I Have... Who Has...?

I have the word:
"LEAVE"

Who has the rhyming word for this name?
My name is Todd.
My 12 toes are really _____.

I Have... Who Has...?

I have the word:
"ODD"

Who has the **FIRST CARD?**

I Have... Who Has...? Rhyming Names Answer Key

	I have...	Who has the rhyming word for this name?
1	I have the FIRST CARD.	My name is Bob. My favorite food is corn on the_____.
2	cob	My name is Jan. I ride around town in my _____.
3	van	My name is Billy. In class I always act _____.
4	silly	My name is Jack. After school I have a _____.
5	snack	My name is Peter. When I'm cold I turn on the _____.
6	heater	My name is Dan. I cook bacon in a _____.
7	pan	My name is Mike. Before breakfast I like to ride my _____.
8	bike	My name is Gary. My pet dog is really _____.
9	hairy	My name is Anna. My favorite fruit is a _____.
10	banana	My name is Drew. I feel sick because I have the _____.
11	flu	My name is Josh. Even though I hate it, my mom makes me eat _____.
12	squash	My name is Scott. I spilled on my shirt so I have a _____.
13	spot	My name is Doug. I like a warm _____.
14	hug	My name is Nancy. My sparkle pants are really _____.
15	fancy	My name is Matt. During class I like to _____.
16	chat	My name is Mary. I like to drink anything that is _____.
17	dairy	My name is Frank. I've never been in a shark _____.
18	tank	My name is Amy. My brother always likes to _____.
19	blame me	My name is Pam. I like to listen to a _____.
20	jam	My name is Jean. My favorite color is lime _____.

	I have...	Who has the rhyming word for this name?
21	green	My name is Carrie. My family lives on the _____.
22	prairie	My name is Jen. I don't go to bed until _____.
23	ten	My name is Tom. In high school I will go to _____.
24	prom	My name is Ken. Sometimes I chase around my pet _____.
25	hen	My name is Rose. When I see a camera, I always _____.
26	pose	My name is Judy. Sometimes I'm cranky and really _____.
27	moody	My name is Fred. I dislike going to _____.
28	bed	My name is Lori. At night before bed I like to hear a _____.
29	story	My name is Jane. I'm really smart and use my _____.
30	brain	My name is Steve. When I tell a bad joke, my friends say to _____.
31	leave	My name is Todd. My 12 toes are really _____.
32	odd	Who has the FIRST CARD?

Create Your Own!

I Have… Who Has…?

I have:

Who has…?

I Have… Who Has…?

I have:

Who has…?

I Have… Who Has…?

I have:

Who has…?

I Have… Who Has…?

I have:

Who has…?

I Have… Who Has…?

I have:

Who has…?

I Have… Who Has…?

I have:

Who has…?

I Have… Who Has…?

I have:

Who has…?

I Have… Who Has…?

I have:

Who has…?

I Have... Who Has...? Answer Key

	I have...	Who has ...?
1		
2		
3		
4		
5		
6		
7		
8		
9		
10		
11		
12		
13		
14		
15		
16		
17		
18		
19		
20		
21		
22		
23		
24		
25		
26		
27		
28		
29		
30		
31		
32		

Videos and
downloadables
are available at
Scholastic.com/
FluencyResources.

CHAPTER 8

Get Families Involved

*"My mother always sang to her children. … 'Wee Willie Winkie's'
song was wonderfully sad when she sang. Soon I was able to
play her my own lullabies…. Ever since I was first read to…
there has never been a line read that I didn't hear. As my eyes
followed the sentence, a voice was saying it silently to me."*

—Eudora Welty

According to the first edition of *The Fluent Reader* by Tim, published in 2003, "… a recent
international study of reading achievement found that parental involvement in children's
reading was the number one predictor of reading achievement worldwide." Since that time,
several studies have confirmed the importance of family involvement in children's literacy
development (Padak & Rasinski, 2006). If we accept the notion that the way to become a
better reader is to read a lot, then expanding each student's reading into the home just
makes good sense.

The basic processes for developing reading fluency—modeling fluent reading, being assisted
by another reader, practicing through repeated reading, and then performing what was
practiced—lend themselves very well to family involvement. Moreover, the kinds of texts that
we feel are ideal for fluency—poems, songs, and the like—are very well suited for families. In
this chapter, we explore ways to involve parents in their children's reading fluency and overall
reading development. We start with the idea of parents modeling fluent reading for their
children by reading to them, and then move on to reading that can be done by parents and
their children together, using songs and poems.

We end this chapter with a fluency program called Fast Start that combines the elements of good fluency instruction into a brief protocol that can easily be implemented at home and supported by the school. The goal of each Fast Start lesson is for children to reach a point where they can independently read a short text with good expression and confidence. For developing readers, especially those who struggle in reading, achieving success with each Fast Start lesson and receiving honest praise for their efforts from parents and other family members makes the program an effective way to bridge school and home.

All parents want their children to achieve success in reading. The problem is, many parents don't know what to do. This chapter provides them with simple, brief activities that will move their children toward fluent reading. And it provides you with home-based activities that allow parents to support the instruction you provide at school.

Strategies

**Fluency Skills
Practiced**

E
Expression

A
Automatic
Word Recognition

R
Rhythm
and Phrasing

S
Smoothness

8.A **Parent Read-Aloud**

Parents choose a book that they and their child will love to hear—a classic book or a new one. When reading aloud to their child, encourage them to focus on expression—how the character talks, feels, etc. When they model how to make meaning while reading, their child will pick up on it for their own reading.

Materials Needed	Book of choice
Grades	1–8
Length of Activity	10–20 minutes
Location	home
Extension Idea	• Read consistently every night to help keep the child excited to hear what will happen next in the story.

8.B **Parent Paired Reading**

Parents and their child work together (ideally on a daily basis) to improve his or her reading. Here's how parent paired reading works:

- Child chooses a book or other type of text that he or she is able to read with some degree of success.

- Parent and child sit side by side and read the text aloud together. Child follows the text with a finger as it is read.

- Parent and child create a nonverbal signal (e.g., tap on the wrist) to be used when he or she wishes to "solo" read. The parent follows along silently until the child signals again for him or her to join in.

- If the child experiences difficulty when reading "solo," the parent immediately rejoins the reading, and parent and child continue reading without interruption for at least 10 minutes.

Materials Needed	Reading material of the child's choice
Grades	1–8
Length of Activity	10–15 minutes
Location	home
Extension Ideas	• After paired reading, encourage parents to examine any words that gave the child difficulty because he or she struggled to decode them and/or understand their meaning. • For more information, see Topping, K. (1987). Paired reading: A powerful technique for parent use. *The Reading Teacher*, 40, 604-614

Fluency Skills Practiced

E
Expression

A
Automatic
Word Recognition

R
Rhythm
and Phrasing

S
Smoothness

**Fluency Skills
Practiced**

E
Expression

A
Automatic
Word Recognition

R
Rhythm
and Phrasing

S
Smoothness

8.C Family Sing-Along

Organize a sing-along for individual families. Make copies of songs that the family is likely to be familiar with or songs for members of earlier generations to teach to members of later generations. If possible, involve multiple generations in the sing-along!

Materials Needed	Songs familiar to the family. You can find song lyrics at various websites such as www.theteachersguide.com/ChildrensSongs.htm.
Grades	1–8
Length of Activity	10–60 minutes
Location	home
Extension Idea	• Have parents practice the songs with their child before the sing-along so he or she will feel successful.

8.D Fast Start Reading

Parents and their child work together each day to read and reread short patterned texts, such as poems. Here's how Fast Start Reading works:

- Parent and child sit side by side with a copy of the chosen text.

- After a brief discussion of the text's content, parent reads it to child several times, pointing to the words as they are read.

- Parent and child then read the text several more times together, with either parent or child pointing to the words as they are read.

- After several readings, child is likely to have the text largely mastered. So parent invites child to read aloud the text several more times. Child may perform the text for other family members who should praise him or her.

- Parent and child engage in a brief study of interesting letters, words, sounds, or phrases in the text.

Materials Needed	A daily nursery rhyme or poem, such as "Little Bo Peep" (pp. 304–305) and "A Song of Sixpence" (pp. 306–307)
Grades	K–3
Length of Activity	15 minutes per day
Location	home
Extension Ideas	• After the child has mastered several poems, urge parents to return to and read previously read poems. • Have parents create a word wall or display of interesting words harvested from each poem, and then read the ever-growing list of words with their child daily. • For more information, see *Fast Start for Early Readers* and *Fast Start: Getting Ready to Read* by Nancy Padak and Timothy V. Rasinski.

Fluency Skills Practiced

E
Expression

A
Automatic Word Recognition

R
Rhythm and Phrasing

S
Smoothness

Name: _____ Date: _____

Little Bo Peep

Little Bo Peep

Has lost her sheep,

And doesn't know where to find them.

Leave them alone,

And they'll come home,

Wagging their tails behind them.

Little Bo Peep

Looking at Words and Letters

☐ **1.** Ask your child to find and circle the *t*'s.

☐ **2.** Ask your child to find and circle the two lines in the poem that have only three words.

☐ **3.** Say, *I'll say two words. You raise your hand if they begin the same:*

little, lost   **peep, bo**   **lost, leave**

☐ **4.** Ask your child to count all the words in the poem.

☐ **5.** Ask your child to point to the top, then the bottom, of the poem.

Playing With Sounds

☐ **1.** Say, *Listen while I clap (or tap) the beats of the poem. Now let's clap (or tap) the beats of the poem together.*

☐ **2.** Ask your child how many beats are in these words: *little* (2), *lost* (1), *leave* (1), *wagging* (2).

☐ **3.** Say, *I'll say two words. Clap your hands if they rhyme:*

alone, them   **sheep, peep**   **come, home**

Beginning to Read

☐ **1.** Ask your child to find and circle words with a long *o*. (*Bo, know, alone, home*)

☐ **2.** Say, *I'll say a word. You tell me the last sound in it:* peep, lost, them, tails.

☐ **3.** Ask your child to find the words with two syllables or beats and to underline them. (*little, doesn't, alone, wagging, behind*)

☐ **4.** Write *sheep* on a sheet of paper. Point out the *–eep* word family. Together, brainstorm, write, and read other words that rhyme and belong to the word family.

☐ **5.** Together, choose two or three words from the poem. Add them to your word wall and practice these words daily. Or add them to your child's word bank (a collection of words on cards, one word per card).

Name: _____   Date: _____

A Song of Sixpence

Sing a song of sixpence,

A pocket full of rye;

Four and twenty blackbirds

Baked in a pie.

When the pie was opened,

The birds began to sing;

Wasn't that a dainty dish

To set before the king?

A Song of Sixpence

Looking at Words and Letters

☐ **1.**   Ask your child to find two lines with four words.

☐ **2.**   Ask your child to find five lines with five words.

☐ **3.**   Say, *Circle uppercase T's and draw boxes around lowercase I's.*

Playing With Sounds

☐ **1.**   Say, *Find three number words. Circle them. Write the numeral for each one.*

☐ **2.**   Say, *Clap your hands if these words start the same.*

☐ **3.**   Say, *I'll say a word. You say one that rhymes. I say, "sing." You say _____.* Repeat with *rye, set, dish, when.*

Beginning to Read

☐ **1.**   Say, *I will say some words. You raise your hand if they have long vowel sounds:* sing, rye, blackbirds, pie, baked, dish, began.

☐ **2.**   Put the following words on slips of paper: *pocket, rye, blackbirds, pie, birds, dish, king.* Ask your child to sort the words: one syllable or two syllables; living things or not living things.

☐ **3.**   Ask your child to tell one thing in the poem that could not be true. Then ask for one thing in the poem that could be true. Ask "Why?" both times.

☐ **4.**   Write *pie* and *sing* on a sheet of paper. Point out the word families *–ie* and *–ing*. Together, brainstorm, write, and read other words that rhyme and belong to the word families. *(die, tie, lie; bring, flight, wing)*

☐ **5.**   Together, choose two or three words from the poem. Add them to your wall and practice these words daily. Or add them to your child's word bank (a collection of words on cards, one word per card).

Videos and downloadables are available at **Scholastic.com/FluencyResources.**

APPENDIX

"You know you will never get to the end of the journey. But this, so far from discouraging, only adds to the joy and glory of the climb."

—Sir Winston Churchill

Teacher Resources

How to Read With Expression

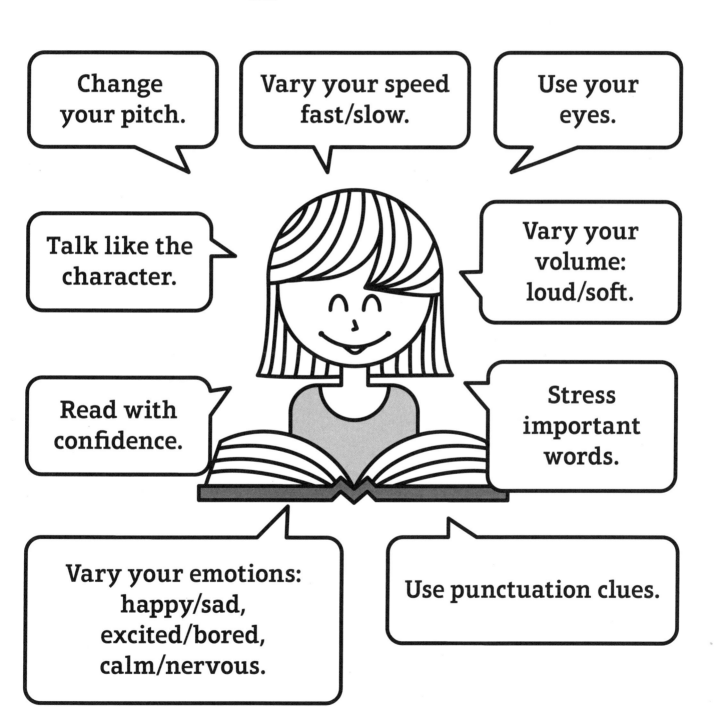

Change your pitch.

Vary your speed fast/slow.

Use your eyes.

Talk like the character.

Vary your volume: loud/soft.

Read with confidence.

Stress important words.

Vary your emotions: happy/sad, excited/bored, calm/nervous.

Use punctuation clues.

Read With

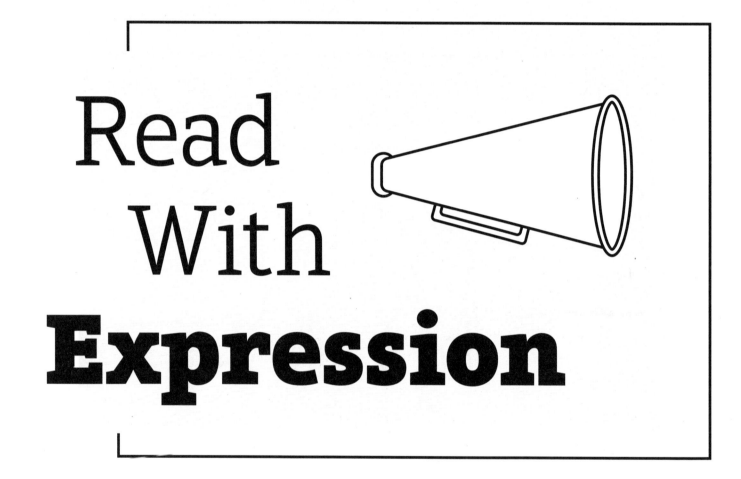

Expression

Watch your volume and tone.
Be confident and natural!

Read With

Automatic Word Recognition

Read effortlessly and at a good pace!

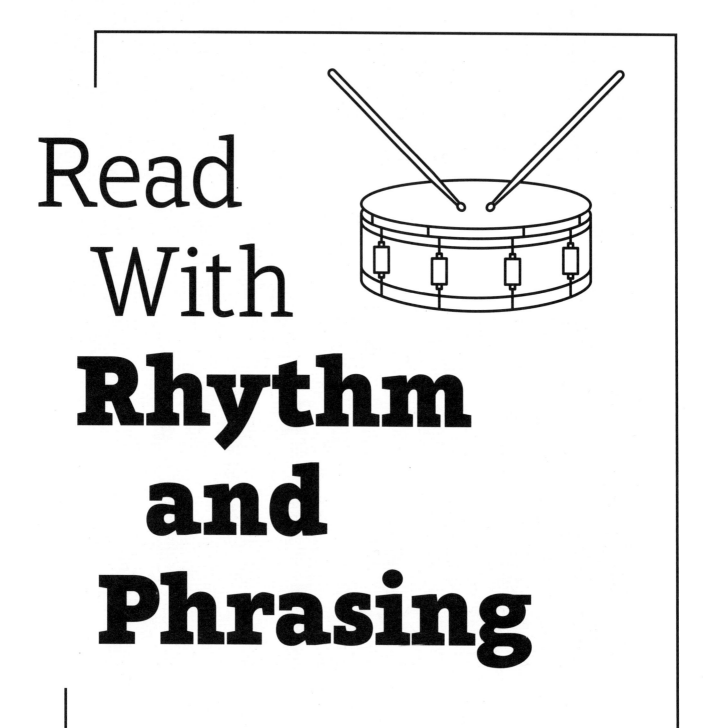

Read With Rhythm and Phrasing

Go phrase by phrase. Pay attention to punctuation. Be easy on the ear!

Read With Smoothness

Smoothness

Sound smooth, go with the flow, and fix mistakes!

Name: _____ Date: _____

Name of Evaluator: _____ Title of Text: _____

Student Fluency Evaluation: EARS

Grades 3–5

Expression

Watch your volume and tone. Be confident and natural!

☐ Reads with no expression.
☐ Reads with a little expression.
☐ Reads with too much expression.
☐ Reads with just-right, meaningful expression.

Automatic Word Recognition

Read effortlessly and at a good pace!

☐ Pace is too slow. Words are not read automatically.
☐ Pace is too fast and does not sound conversational.
☐ Reads words automatically, at the right pace.

Rhythm and Phrasing

Go phrase by phrase. Pay attention to punctuation. Be easy on the ear!

☐ Reading is choppy.
☐ Reads in awkward word chunks.
☐ Reads with few or no breaks.
☐ Reads with rhythm, phrase by phrase.

Smoothness

Sound smooth, go with the flow, and fix mistakes!

☐ Struggles with a lot of words.
☐ Knows some words, but not all.
☐ Knows most words and fixes mistakes. Reading is smooth!

Name of Reader: _____   Name of Evaluator: _____

Title of Text: _____

Student Fluency Evaluation: EARS

Grades 6–8

Choose the box that best describes the reading done by the reader.

Expression

Watch your volume and tone. Be confident and natural!

4	3	2	0–1
Expression is consistent and varied. Reading sounds natural and confident.	Expression is mostly consistent and varied. Reading sounds natural and confident for the most part.	Expression is inconsistent. There is only some variation and confidence in the reading.	There is little to no expression and a monotone voice.

Automatic Word Recognition

Read effortlessly and at a good pace!

4	3	2	0–1
Reads words automatically, effortlessly, and at a consistent pace.	Reads most words automatically and at a consistent pace.	Reads some words automatically, at a slow pace at times.	Reads few words automatically, at a very slow pace.

Rhythm and Phrasing

Go phrase by phrase. Pay attention to punctuation. Be easy on the ear!

4	3	2	0–1
Reads in phrases or chunks and pays attention to intonation using punctuation and text clues.	Reads with some choppiness, but in phrases or chunks. Pays attention to intonation somewhat, using punctuation and text clues.	Reads in frequent short or choppy phrases. Intonation is inconsistent or sounds "off" when punctuation and text clues are used.	Reads in a choppy, word-by-word manner. Intonation sounds "off" when punctuation and text clues are used.

Smoothness

Sound smooth, go with the flow, and fix mistakes!

4	3	2	0–1
Reads words smoothly and accurately, with minimal or no hesitation.	Reads most words smoothly and accurately, but with some hesitation.	Struggles to read some words accurately and smoothly. Hesitations interfere with flow.	Frequently struggles to read words inaccurately. Hesitations are constant.

Multidimensional Fluency Scale

	4 Excelling	3 Proficient	2 Approaching	1 Developing
E Expression ✓ expression matches meaning ✓ varied volume, intonation, and tone ✓ reads with confidence ✓ natural sounding	• consistently uses expression through varied intonation, volume, and tone to match meaning • reads with confidence • is natural-sounding and easy to understand	• mostly uses expression by sometimes varying intonation, volume, and tone to match meaning • shows confidence but inconsistently • is mostly natural-sounding and easy to understand	• attempts expression, but is inconsistent and often does not match the meaning • lacks confidence, reads quietly • primarily focuses on saying the words correctly	• pays minimal or no attention to expression • reads in a quiet and monotone voice • reads words as if simply to get them out
A Automatic Word Recognition ✓ reads automatically ✓ reads effortlessly ✓ pace matches text (rate)	• reads nearly all words automatically and effortlessly • uses a pace that is consistently conversational and appropriate for the nature of the text • number of words read per minute matches grade-level requirement. See "Target Fluency Ranges" table on page 16	• reads most words automatically and effortlessly • uses a mixture of conversational and slow reading • number of words read per minute meets grade-level requirement. See "Target Fluency Ranges" table on page 16	• does not read most words automatically and has to stop to recognize words • reads at a moderately slow pace • number of words read per minute is below grade-level requirement. See "Target Fluency Ranges" table on page 16	• does not read words automatically and has to stop frequently to recognize words • reads at an excessively slow and laborious pace • number of words read is well below grade-level requirement. See "Target Fluency Ranges" table on page 16
R Rhythm and Phrasing ✓ reads phrase-by-phrase chunks" ✓ attention to punctuation with intonation and pauses ✓ easy to listen to	• reads primarily in phrases, chunks, and sentence units • pays attention to intonation and pauses at punctuation consistently and accurately	• reads with some choppiness, but is generally able to go phrase by phrase • pays attention to intonation and usually pauses at punctuation consistently and accurately	• reads in two- and three-word phrases frequently • reads with choppiness • often exhibits improper intonation and pauses at punctuation	• reads word by word frequently • reads in a monotonic manner • shows little sense of phrase boundaries • exhibits improper intonation and pauses at punctuation
S Smoothness ✓ smooth-sounding with flow ✓ accurate word recognition ✓ minimal hesitations ✓ self-corrects	• reads nearly all words accurately • reads smoothly, with minimal hesitations • has few word and structure difficulties and corrects quickly	• reads most words accurately • breaks occasionally from smoothness and hesitates • has a few difficulties with specific words and/or structures, but they do not impede overall flow	• struggles to read words accurately • pauses and hesitates frequently at "rough spots" in text, which disrupts the overall flow	• requires frequent assistance for inaccuracies: long pauses, insertions, mispronunciation, omissions, false starts, sound-outs, repetitions • is unaware of mistakes

Professional References

Allington, R. L. (1983). Fluency: The neglected reading goal. *The Reading Teacher, 36,* 556–561.

Chard, D. J., Vaughn, S., & Tyler, B. (2002). A synthesis of research on effective interventions for building fluency with elementary students with learning disabilities. *Journal of Learning Disabilities, 35,* 386–406.

Dowhower, S. L. (1994). Repeated reading revisited: Research into practice. *Reading and Writing Quarterly, 10,* 343–358.

Duke, N. K., Pressley, M., & Hilden, K. (2004). Difficulties in reading comprehension. In C. A. Stone, E. R. Silliman, B. J. Ehren, and K. Apel (Eds.), *Handbook of language and literacy; Development and disorders,* pp. 501–520. New York: Guilford.

Kuhn, M. R., Schwanenflugel, P. J., & Meisinger, E. B. (2010). Review of Research: Aligning Theory and Assessment of Reading Fluency: Automaticity, Prosody, and Definitions of Fluency. *Reading Research Quarterly, 45*(2), 230–251.

Kuhn, M. R., Schwanenflugel, P., Morris, R., Morrow, L, Woo, D., Meisinger, E., Sevcik, R., Bradley, B., & Stahl, S. (2006). Teaching children to become fluent and automatic readers. *Journal of Literacy Research, 38,* 357–387.

Kuhn, M. R., & Stahl, S. A. (2003). Fluency: A review of developmental and remedial practices. *Journal of Educational Psychology, 95,* 3–21.

National Governors Association and Council of Chief School Officers (2016). *Common Core State Standards.* Downloaded from www.corestandards.org

National Reading Panel. (2000). *Report of the National Reading Panel: Teaching children to read. Report of the subgroups.* Washington, DC: U.S. Department of Health and Human Services, National Institutes of Health.

Padak, N., & Rasinski, T. (2005). *Fast start for early readers: A research-based, send-home literacy Program.* New York: Scholastic.

Padak, N., & Rasinski, T. (2008). *Fast start: Getting ready to read.* New York: Scholastic.

Paige, D. D., Rasinski, T. V., & Magpuri-Lavell, T. (2012). Is fluent, expressive reading important for high school readers? *Journal of Adolescent & Adult Literacy, 56*(1), 67–76.

Paige, D. D., Rasinski, T. V., Magpuri-Lavell, T., & Smith, G. (2014). Interpreting the relationships among prosody, automaticity, accuracy and silent reading comprehension in secondary students. *Journal of Literacy Research, 46*(2), 123–156.

Rasinski, T. V. (2005). The role of the teacher in effective fluency instruction. *New England Reading Association Journal, 41,* 9–12.

Rasinski, T. V. (2006). Reading fluency instruction: Moving beyond accuracy, automaticity, and prosody. *The Reading Teacher, 59,* 704–706.

Rasinski, T. V. (2010). *The fluent reader: Oral and silent reading strategies for building word recognition, fluency, and comprehension* (2nd edition). New York: Scholastic.

Rasinski, T. V. (2012). Why reading fluency should be hot. *The Reading Teacher, 65,* 516–522.

Rasinski, T. V. (2017). Readers who struggle: Why many struggle and a modest proposal for improving their reading. *The Reading Teacher, 70*(5), 519–524. doi: 10.1002/trtr.1533

Rasinski, T. V., & Padak, N. D. (1998). How elementary students referred for compensatory reading instruction perform on school-based measures of word recognition, fluency, and comprehension. *Reading Psychology: An International Quarterly, 19,* 185–216.

Rasinski, T. V., & Padak, N. (2005). *3-minute reading assessments: word recognition, fluency, and comprehension for grades 1–4.* New York: Scholastic.

Rasinski, T. V., & Padak, N. (2005). *3-minute reading assessments: word recognition, fluency, and Comprehension for grades 5–8.* New York: Scholastic

Rasinski, T. V., Padak, N., McKeon, C., Krug,-Wilfong, L., Friedauer, J., & Heim, P. (2005) Is reading fluency a key for successful high school reading? *Journal of Adolescent and Adult Literacy, 49,* 22–27.

Rasinski, T. V., Reutzel, C. R., Chard, D. & Linan-Thompson, S. (2011). Reading fluency. In M. L. Kamil, P. D. Pearson, B. Moje, & P. Afflerbach (Eds), *Handbook of Reading Research, Volume IV* (pp. 286–319). New York: Routledge.

Rasinski, T. V., Rikli, A., & Johnston, S. (2009). Reading fluency: More than automaticity? More than a concern for the primary grades? *Literacy Research and Instruction, 48,* 350–361.

Rasinski, T. V., Yildirim, K. & Nageldinger, J. (2011), Building fluency through the phrased text lesson. *The Reading Teacher, 65*: 252–255. doi: 10.1002/TRTR.01036

Samuels, S. J. (1979). The method of repeated readings. *The Reading Teacher, 32,* 403–408.

Samuels, S. J. (2007). The DIBELS tests: Is speed of barking at print what we mean by fluency? *Reading Research Quarterly, 42,* 563–566.

Stevens, E., Walker, M., & Vaughn, S. (2017). The effects of reading fluency interventions on the reading fluency and reading comprehension performance of elementary students with reading disabilities: A synthesis of research from 2001 to 2014. *Journal of Learning Disabilities, 50,* 576–590.

Topping, K. (1987a). Paired reading: A powerful technique for parent use. *The Reading Teacher, 40,* 604–614.

Topping, K. (1987b). Peer tutored paired reading: Outcome data from ten projects. *Educational Psychology, 7,* 133–145.

Topping, K. (1989). Peer tutoring and paired reading. Combining two powerful techniques. *The Reading Teacher, 42,* 488–494.

Valencia, S. W., & Buly, M. R. (2004). Behind test scores: What struggling readers really need. *The Reading Teacher, 57,* 520–531.

Zutell, J. & Rasinski, T. V. (1991). Training teachers to attend to their students' oral reading fluency. *In Theory to Practice, 30,* 211–217.

Children's Books Cited

Banyai, I. (1995). *Zoom*. New York: Viking Books for Young Readers.

Banyai, I. (1998). *Re-zoom*. New York: Puffin Books.

Blackall, S. (2007). *Knock, knock*. New York: Dial.

Brown, M. W. (2007). *Goodnight moon*. New York: HarperFestival.

Colandro, L. (2014). *There was an old lady who swallowed a fly* (series). Cartwheel.

Cole, J. (1989). *Anna Bananna: 101 jump-rope rhymes*. New York: HarperCollins.

Cronin, D. (2000). *Click, clack, moo: Cows that type*. New York: Atheneum Books for Young Readers.

Cronin, D. (2002). *Giggle, giggle, quack*. New York: Atheneum Books for Young Readers.

Cronin, D. (2003). *Diary of a worm*. New York: HarperCollins.

Cronin, D. (2006). *Dooby, dooby, moo*. New York: Atheneum Books for Young Readers.

Cronin, D. (2008). *Thump, quack, moo*. New York: Atheneum Books for Young Readers.

Cronin, D. (2013). *Diary of a fly*. New York: HarperCollins.

Cronin, D. (2013). *Diary of a spider*. New York: HarperCollins.

dePaola, T. (1978). *Pancakes for breakfast*. New York: HMH Books for Young Readers.

Fawcett, G., Harrison, D. & Rasinski, T. (2009). *Partner poems for building fluency*. New York: Scholastic.

Fleischman, P. (1989). *I am phoenix: Poems for two voices*. New York: HarperCollins.

Fleischman, P. (2005). *Joyful noise: Poems for two voices*. New York: HarperCollins.

Fleischman, P. (2008). *Big talk: Poems for four voices*. New York: Candlewick.

Franco, B. (2009). *Messing around on the monkey bars: And other school poems for two voices*. New York: Candlewick.

Geisert, A. (2013). *Thunderstorm*. Brooklyn: Enchanted Lion Books.

Gerber, C. (2013). *Seeds, bees, butterflies, and more! Poems for two voices*. New York: Henry Holt.

Hoberman, M. (2006). *You read to me, I'll read to you: Very short stories to read together*. New York: Little, Brown.

Hoberman, M. (2012). *You read to me, I'll read to you: Very short fables to read together*. New York: Little, Brown.

Hoberman, M. (2013). *You read to me, I'll read to you: Very short fairy tales to read together*. New York: Little, Brown.

Katz, A. (2001). *Take me out of the bathtub and other silly dilly songs*. New York: Margaret K. McElderry Books.

Katz, A. (2003). *I'm still here in the bathtub: Brand new silly dilly songs*. New York: Margaret K. McElderry Books.

Katz, A. (2006). *Are you quite polite?* New York: Margaret K. McElderry Books.

Katz, A. (2008). *Where did they hide my presents? Silly dilly christmas songs*. New York: Margaret K. McElderry Books.

Katz, A. (2009). *Going, going, gone! And other silly dilly sports songs*. New York: Margaret K. McElderry Books.

Katz, A. (2010). *Smelly locker: Silly dilly school songs*. New York: Margaret K. McElderry Books.

Katz, B. (2007). *Partner poems for building fluency, grades 2–4*. New York: Scholastic.

Lehman, B. (2004). *The red book*. New York: HMH Books for Young Readers.

Lobel, A. (1979). *Frog and toad together*. New York: HarperCollins.

Lobel, A. (1984). *Frog and toad all year*. New York: HarperCollins.

Lobel, A. (2003). *Frog and toad are friends*. New York: HarperCollins.

Lobel, A. (2004). *Days with frog and toad*. New York: HarperCollins.

Martin Jr., B. (1997). *Polar bear, polar bear, what do you hear?* New York: Henry Holt.

Martin Jr., B. (2006). *Panda bear, panda bear, what do you see?* New York: Henry Holt.

Martin Jr., B. (2007). *Brown bear, brown bear, what do you see?* New York: Puffin Books.

Numeroff, L. (1991). *If you give a moose a muffin*. New York: HarperCollins.

Numeroff, L. (1998). *If you give a pig a pancake*. New York: HarperCollins.

Numeroff, L. (2015). *If you give a mouse a cookie* (series). New York: HarperCollins.

Pinkney, J. (2009). *The lion and the mouse*. New York: Little, Brown Books for Young Readers.

Pottle, R. (2007). *I'm allergic to school!: Funny poems and songs about school*. Minnetonka: Meadowbrook Press.

Prater, J. (2000). *Again*. Hauppauge: Barrons Juveniles.

Raschka, C. (2000). *Ring! Yo?* Richard Jackson Books.

Raschka, C. (2007). *Yo! Yes?* New York: Scholastic.

Rathmann, P. (1996). *Good night, gorilla*. New York: G.P. Putnam's Sons Books for Young Readers.

Shannon, D. (1998). *No, david!* New York: Blue Sky Press.

Shannon, D. (1999). *David gets in trouble*. New York: Blue Sky Press.

Shannon, D. (1999). *David goes to school*. New York: Blue Sky Press.

Thomson, B. (2010). *Chalk*. Seattle: Two Lions.

Thomson, B. (2013). *Fossil*. Seattle: Two Lions.

Viorst, J. (1987). *Alexander and the terrible, horrible, no good, very bad day*. New York: Atheneum Books for Young Readers.

Viorst, J. (1987). *Alexander, who used to be rich last Sunday*. London: Silver Burdett.

Viorst, J. (1998). *Alexander, who's not (do you hear me? I mean it!) going to move*. London: Silver Burdett.

Waddell, M. (2002). *Owl babies*. New York: Candlewick.

Wiesner, D. (2006). *Flotsam*. New York: Clarion Books.

Wiesner, D. (2011). *Tuesday*. New York: HMH Books for Young Readers.

Williams, S. (1996). *I went walking*. New York: Houghton Mifflin Harcourt.

Willems, M. (2004). *The pigeon finds a hot dog!* New York: Scholastic.

Willems, M. (2004). *Don't let the pigeon drive the bus!* London: Walker Books.

Willems, M. (2005). *The pigeon has feelings, too!* Burbank, CA: Disney.

Willems, M. (2006). *Don't let the pigeon stay up late!* Burbank, CA: Disney.

Willems, M. (2008). *The pigeon wants a puppy!* Burbank, CA: Disney.

Willems, M. (2012). *The pigeon needs a bath!* London: Walker Books.

Wilson, K. (2005). *Bear snores on*. New York: Little Simon.

General Index

Index of Texts Used in Strategy Pages